# "MOM, HE HIT ME!"

# "Mom, he hit me!"

## WHAT TO DO ABOUT SIBLING RIVALRY

## Elaine K. McEwan

Harold Shaw Publishers
Wheaton, Illinois

Scripture quotation on page 22 is taken from *The Jerusalem Bible,* copyright © 1966 by Darton, Longman & Todd, Ltd. and Doubleday, a division of Bantam Doubleday Dell Publishing Group, Inc. Reprinted by permission.

ISBN 0-87788-556-7

Edited by Diane Eble

Cover design by David LaPlaca

---

**Library of Congress Cataloging-in-Publication Data**

McEwan, Elaine K.
   "Mom, he hit me!" : what to do about sibling rivalry / Elaine K. McEwan.
    p.  cm.
  ISBN 0-87788-556-7
  1. Child rearing.  2. Sibling rivalry.  3. Child psychology.
4. Brothers and sisters.  5. Parent and child.  I. Title.
HQ769.M165  1996
649'.1—dc20

                                          96-19241
                                          CIP

---

03  02  01  00  99  98  97  96

10  9  8  7  6  5  4  3  2  1

# Contents

# 1
# Is Sibling Rivalry Normal?

**S**ibling rivalry first reared its ugly head at our house when Emily was three and Patrick was just learning to sit up. We were in our family room on a sunny winter day, the perfect picture of a close-knit family. Out of the blue, my adorable little daughter reached over and gave her brother a hearty shove. His rotund little body toppled toward the fireplace, and his forehead struck the corner of the concrete hearth. His tender skin split open immediately, and as Emily and I watched in horror, blood ran down his face. Everyone began to cry at that point, including me. I wanted to believe it was an accident, but deep down I knew that Emily's actions were precipitated by jealousy at all the attention her new brother was receiving from Mom and Dad. At the age of twenty-five Emily doesn't remember the feelings that preceded the push she gave her brother, but she does remember our trip to the doctor and the stitches Patrick received. And her brother won't let her forget it either. He loves to point out the scar to her in the heat of grown-up sibling battles.

In those early years, I was chagrined that I hadn't done a better job of helping my daughter love her baby brother. My husband and I had read every parenting book on the market and just knew our children would be perfect. We spent exactly the same amount of money on Christmas toys for each child and even went so far as to give them identical stuffed animals. No one would be able to accuse us of playing favorites. But we didn't succeed in stamping out sibling rivalry. Even today, my "twenty-somethings" can still "mix it up" over petty issues and bruise each other's egos. But the prognosis is not all bad. I'm encouraged by the frequent phone calls they make to one another from distant cities, the thoughtful Christmas gifts they exchanged last year, and the admiration they exhibit for one another's achievements. There *is* light at the end of the tunnel.

## What is sibling rivalry?

If Mom and Dad weren't around from the start, would siblings still have rivalry? Maybe, but probably not. The word *rivalry* in the term "sibling rivalry" suggests that two or more individuals are in some kind of competition for a prize. In the case of sibling rivalry, the competitors are brothers and sisters, and the prize is love, attention, and recognition from Mom and Dad. Sometimes even when Mom and Dad have passed on to glory, siblings are still reenacting those timeless battles, perhaps hoping for some kind of posthumous parental accolade. We desperately want to be

Numero Uno and would somehow like to eliminate all contenders.

## Is sibling rivalry normal?

Sibling rivalry is a natural part of family life that, while disconcerting for most parents, is a way for children to learn how to cope with their own greed and jealousy and surmount the petty meanness that comes with all of us as original equipment. Everyone is born wanting the birthright, and rare is the child who arrives selfless enough to willingly share the pie with other hungry mouths. For those who may still be viewing the world through rose-colored glasses, wake up. Sibling rivalry comes with the parenting territory.

A child's first fights arise from rivalry over objects, territory, and parental affection.[1] But don't give up. There is hope. And there are even some positive aspects to sibling rivalry. Learning how to get along with siblings can help a child get ready for one of life's harsher realities: one can't always have all of the advantages or attention one wants. Healthier sibling relationships can and will develop when parents systematically model respect, love, problem solving, and conflict resolution. And sometimes when parents pull back, siblings do very well on their own. In one study, parents left siblings alone in an unfamiliar room with an adult stranger. In more than half of the pairs, the older children (average age of three-and-a-half years) acted to "reassure and comfort their younger siblings (average age of fourteen months) in the absence of the mother. . . ."[2] Taking a proactive, rather than reactive, stance can help your children overcome many of their natural instincts. But if parents ignore sibling rivalry or handle it poorly, the battles will only grow worse—often resulting in total estrangement.

Do be realistic, however. Sibling rivalry will probably never be totally eliminated from a family, but it can be managed, facilitated, and moderated.

## What are the natural causes of sibling rivalry?

Psychologists and researchers who describe sibling rivalry in academic terms talk about frustrated dependency needs and competition with respect to garnering parental and extrafamilial recognition and approval. But it really all boils down to our selfish and sinful natures. We want to be the first and only in the love and lives of our parents, and some of us will go to any length to establish our turf. Jealousy, resentment, and anger are the inborn, natural causes of sibling rivalry. We seem to arrive on the scene with little meters ticking in our brains that are constantly measuring the amount of beauty, talent, privilege, and attention accorded to our siblings. *You are loved more. You are prettier. You are better in sports. You have more privileges. You get more attention from Mom and Dad.* Sometimes the commentary may even be subconscious, so the resentment and hostility don't emerge full blown until young adulthood.

Relative position in the family also serves to create natural sibling rivalry. First-born high achievers and pampered youngest children can frequently take center stage, leaving the often overlooked middle child struggling for recognition and rewards. Questions like *Why do they like the others better than me? How can I make them love me as much as my brother or sister?* and *Why don't they treat me like the others?* fan the fires of sibling rivalry. Or a favored older child can suddenly lose status as a newer member joins the family group.

I had my first brush with sibling rivalry when I was eleven. My brother, four years younger than I, wasn't a problem. My parents did an admirable job of making me feel special when he arrived. And my grandparents and aunts and uncles still accorded me first place in their hearts. So at the ripe old age of ten, no one worried about preparing me for the arrival of a new baby. My mother had a difficult pregnancy, and she had little time to indulge my whims. To add insult to injury, I was expected to help around the house. I resented this infringement on the time I usually spent curled up with a good book. I didn't like taking care of "this bratty, whiny kid."

I still remember the afternoon my mother sent me to fetch my sister; she was about three at the time. She was playing in the sandbox with our next-door neighbor cousins. I ordered her to follow me home in a somewhat imperious tone. She refused. I yelled at her again. She started to cry. I grabbed her by the arm and jerked it vigorously, dragging her across the vacant lot that separated our homes. Her crying grew more desperate. By the time we reached the back door, she was screaming hysterically that her arm was broken. A trip to the emergency room followed (fortunately there was nothing really wrong), and I was grounded for what seemed like the rest of my life. I blush with embarrassment at the retelling of this story. Surely I should have been more gracious and loving and kind. But I wasn't. I was downright mean and nasty. Jealousy and resentment overrode the lessons so faithfully learned at my parents' knees and in Sunday school.

The size of the family is also a factor that can influence the kind and amount of sibling rivalry that is present. With just two or three children in a family, the rivalry between them can be intense. In larger families, while there may seem more opportunities for rivalry, there are also more chances for bonding. Although there were nine siblings in my husband's family, they naturally divided themselves into the "big kids" and the "little kids." Resources were scarce, but there was plenty of discipline and love to go around, and their memories of pulling together in the tough times are inspiring.

## What parental mistakes make sibling rivalry worse?

We as parents often exacerbate situations that are already less than ideal by committing what I call "minor errors in judgment." See if you're guilty of any of the following:

**Playing favorites.** We have a parental favorite. We identify with one child more than any of the others. Perhaps the child who is most like us or the one who makes us proudest will claim first place in our hearts. And then, to make matters worse, we chart a course of action who makes it clear to everyone just how we feel.

**Assigning labels.** We berate or complain about one or more of our children within their hearing. I often witnessed this mistake as parents came to enroll multiple children in the elementary school of which I was principal for many years. I would cringe to hear parents describe one child as the "smart one," another as the "troublemaker," and still a third as the child who "needs a lot of help." I could almost see the "smart one" preen as the others shot darts of resentment in their sibling's direction.

**Holding a trial.** We act as judge and jury whenever our children are fighting or disagreeing and feel compelled to come down with a verdict of who is right or wrong. Instead, we should help our children to resolve their own conflicts.

**Comparing kids.** We compare our children with each other and fan the fires of jealousy. Parents who believe they will instill desirable habits and behavior in one child by pointing out the stellar qualities of another are setting themselves up for problems, both short- and long-term. Comparison is an insidious destroyer of self-esteem. Kids do enough of it on their own without our help.

**Choosing by gender.** We emphasize sex differences. Mom always takes the side of the girls, or Dad votes with the boys.

**Making spies.** We reward tattling and thus encourage it.

**Skating on the surface.** We don't look for the real reasons kids fight. We often do not recognize that a dispute may be unrelated to the surface problem, so we fail to go deeper.

**Rejecting imperfections.** We expect perfection and are far too punitive and unrealistic about our expectations for harmony between siblings.

**Taking sides.** We let our kids drive a wedge between us and our spouses. We take sides with our kids.

**Avoiding what is unpleasant.** We put our heads in the sand and refuse to talk about rivalry, communication problems, or minor disputes.

**Fostering competition.** We foster competition rather than cooperation in our families. In business settings, too much competition gives people headaches, stomachaches, and backaches. They become more anxious, more suspicious, and more hostile. The same things can happen in our homes.

**Creating conflict.** We create an insecure home environment through family conflict, disunity, and disharmony. Children become easily upset by family disequilibrium; their uneasiness and disquietude will be reflected in how they behave toward each other. Increased rivalry and fighting between siblings can be a reflection of increased parental tension.

**Overstressing equality.** We fail to allow for differences (temperaments, gifts, talents, and personalities) in our children and try to treat them all "equally." I personally found it very hard to give up the notion that in order to be fair you must give equally in terms of things, amount, time, and even love. Yet I came to understand that giving unequally, according to individual needs (especially at specific times), is a better way. Rather than claiming equal love, show each of your children how he or she is loved uniquely. Love is not (or shouldn't be) a limited resource in your family. We should always have plenty to go around.

**Being inconsistent.** We are genuinely unfair and inconsistent. We waffle regarding our positions on things. Children expect to be treated today the same way they were treated yesterday. Yes, rules can change. Kids get older. At that point, be clear in the reasons for the changes. Broken promises are also unfair. Of course, there are times when illness or emergency will keep you from fulfilling a pledge you made to a child, but don't let it happen often or you will create anger and hostility in your children.

**Assigning roles.** We cast our children into well-defined and specific roles, building up one child at the expense of another. Don't build up the gifts and abilities of one child by making sure that no other child has a chance to succeed in the same arena. Emily was always the "artist" in our family, and we unconsciously featured her in this role *ad nauseum*. During his high school years, Patrick was able to take a complete battery of aptitude tests which rated his spatial/artistic abilities in the ninety-ninth percentile. "But I'm not the artistic one," he argued with the counselor who was explaining the results to us. "My sister is the artist."

The wise counselor went on to explain that artistic abilities can take many forms, and his ability to lay out an award-winning school newspaper was just as "artistic" as his sister's ability to produce a detailed drawing.

**Shirking supervision.** We make four major mistakes in providing supervision and discipline:

- We give too much too soon. We are much too punitive in reaction to sibling rivalry. Ignore some stuff and recognize that developmental milestones will take care of a lot of sibling rivalry.

- We're too late with too little in our supervision and management of sibling rivalry. We may inadvertently reward obnoxious behavior, failing to set limits and provide structure and expectations for our children.

- We feel guilty because we can't stand our kids' behavior or because we haven't been "perfect parents," and thus waffle in our approach to managing conflict in our families. Our inconsistency causes even more rivalry.

- We disagree with our spouses about discipline and argue with each other in front of the kids.

## What are the critical periods when sibling rivalry may be at its worst?

There are several critical periods in the life of a child when sibling rivalry may be strong. The birth of a new baby is traditionally a time when parents are on the lookout for signs of problems. Dozens of books and articles have been written about how to get your child ready for a new addition to the family. But middle childhood (ages 6-12) is also a critical period in which children are actively engaged in vying for their special place in the family. I personally believe that whenever the family structure changes, siblings once again redefine their roles. It is often at this time that old rivalries, grudges, and conflicts bubble to the surface and cause family members to wonder if kids ever do "grow up."

My children were both in college when their father was diagnosed with terminal cancer. Two years apart in age, they had only been at home together for brief vacation periods. They were mature, helpful, supportive, and patient during the final month we spent together as a family. We took turns caring for my husband's physical needs at home and spelled each other at his bedside. I secretly took pride in their consideration for me and for each other. After their father died, however, they decided it was time to renegotiate their relationships with each other and with me. Just when I was at my lowest ebb, they decided to take each other on. My conflict resolution and negotiation skills got a major workout.

There was another flare-up of jealousy and anger when I decided to remarry. The rules of the game were once again changing, and roles needed to be redefined. "Yes," I reassured them, "there's room in my life for everyone. I'll still love you even after I've remarried." Sibling rivalry can be a major problem when two families are blended. See chapter 6 for information and suggestions on how to handle this special situation.

## What are the best ways to handle sibling rivalry?

Some parents think they'll solve the sibling rivalry problem by having only one child. There's a certain logic to this reasoning, but conventional wisdom and even some psychological research says that it's good for a child to have siblings. Siblings, they say, create certain stresses which, if overcome successfully, will give your child resources that can be adapted to deal with other situations later in life. Supposedly, siblings help us learn how to share, learn how to come face to face with our own greed and jealousy, and especially how to accept our own individuality. Siblings are companions for each other, and in spite of the hostilities that sometimes arise, they are often quick to come to each other's aid when an outside aggressor threatens.

This sounds wonderful, but in far too many families, parents fail to recognize the potential for good in sibling rivalry and fall apart at the seams when it first becomes apparent. They make all the mistakes listed earlier and more and then wring their hands in despair when family reunions resemble Civil War battles more than Norman Rockwell paintings. The chapters ahead will give you dozens of specific suggestions for how to manage sibling rivalry and facilitate communication and conflict resolution in your family, but here's a short course to get you started.

**Create a family team.** Do you encourage shared decision making and cooperative family activities? Help your kids take responsibility for their actions? Build both group and individual accountability? Do you facilitate open lines of communication between family members and model conflict resolution on a daily basis? If you need help with establishing the feeling of "team" in your family, then check out chapter 2.

**Study uniqueness.** Can you list the gifts, talents, and strengths of each of your children? Do you make each of your children feel special and unique? Do you spend time alone with each child listening to joys and frustrations? Consult chapter 3 for some ideas about how to "get in tune" with your child's uniqueness.

**Take personal inventory.** Check out your own behavior. Often, if you want to change your kids' behavior, you will need to start with your own. Do you have a limited repertoire of things to do when your kids start fighting? Do you feel like screaming (and frequently do) when your kids draw battle lines? Are you playing favorites, interfering too much, or out of harmony with your spouse? Take an inventory, and if you need help, use some of the strategies in chapter 4.

**Nurture family.** Do you let your kids express their feelings? Do you take a proactive stance and spend time helping your children become nurturing, supportive siblings? Dozens of ways to nurture a supportive and caring family structure are provided in chapter 5.

**Consider special needs.** Do you have special circumstances in your family that seem to work against positive sibling relationships? A child with a disability or Attention Deficit Disorder? A blended family with multiple stepsiblings? Turn to chapter 6 for ways to manage sibling rivalry in your "special" family situation.

### Endnotes

1. W. W. Hartrup, "Aggression in Childhood: Development Perspectives," *American Psychologist* 5 (1974): 336-41.

2. R. B. Stewart, "Sibling attachment relationships: Child-infant interactions in the strange situation," *Developmental Psychology* 19 (1983): 192-99.

# 2

# Teamwork: Building a Family That Works Together

**T**eamwork is a buzzword in the business and athletic world, but the team model is less frequently accepted or nurtured in families where some parents still believe that the mantle of parental responsibility means they must "do it all." Parents can wear themselves out trying to be the all-knowing, all-wise, bountiful providers for their children. And children can come to expect parents to protect them from all of the realities of life, meet their every need, and be responsible for everything that happens to them. I'd like to recommend a family system based on the team concept. That doesn't mean that parents abdicate their leadership roles or turn over decisions to their children. But it does mean sharing some of the decisions and developing a shared sense of responsibility. Organizing a family around the concept of teamwork fosters characteristics such as:

- Commitment: a willingness to put family goals above individual ones
- Trust: a feeling of confidence and support on the part of family members for each other
- Purpose: an understanding of what the family's mission is (see sample below)
- Communication: the ability to handle conflict, decision making, and day-to-day interaction
- Involvement: partnership and ownership in the family's mission

Parenting for teamwork is neither permissive nor authoritarian. It is mutual. It means working together so that no one either wins or loses. Parents don't make all the decisions, but neither do they cave in and let children run roughshod over their needs, values, and interests.

The Apostle Paul put it this way in Ephesians 4:15-16:

If we live by the truth and in love, we shall grow in all ways into Christ, who is the head by whom the whole body is fitted and joined together, every joint adding its own strength, for each separate part to work according to its function. So the body grows until it has built itself up, in love. (JB)

If you want to build a team atmosphere in your family, you will need to do four things:

- Develop your own family vision and mission statement.
- Appreciate and affirm the uniqueness of each of your children (see chapter 3).
- Implement a structure for dealing with the day-to-day operation of your family team similar to the family council described in the pages ahead.
- Implement certain processes and activities on a regular basis (see chapters 4 and 5).

## Your Family's Mission Statement

Vision and mission statements are commonly found in schools, businesses, and churches, but you might not have thought they were important for a family. The terms *mission* and *vision* are often used interchangeably, but I believe they are different. I define *vision* as a driving force reflecting the parents' image of the future based on their values, beliefs, and experiences. Vision is your personal view of what you would like your family to become. *Mission,* on the other hand, is the direction that emerges from the vision that guides the day-to-day behavior of your family. The mission, in order to be fully realized, must be developed collectively with other family members. Developing a family mission statement can only be done when children are old enough to understand and discuss abstract concepts like teamwork, individuality, cooperation, authority, and responsibility. But early elementary children have the beginning understandings of these ideas and can help the family develop a mission statement.

Ideally, the development of a family vision statement would begin before a couple have any children at all. I've included a sample of one family's vision statement below. You can see that each of the statements carries with it an entire set of values and beliefs that will drive the operation of the family. These beliefs will govern day-to-day actions, decisions, and expenditures. Conflict between parents regarding any of these important statements could cause family dysfunction, ineffective parenting, and possibly even dissolution. So you can see how important it will be to agree on your family vision statement. As you read the one that follows, keep in mind that it is just an example. It's not the right one or the only one.

- Our family affirms the uniqueness and individuality of each family member.
- Our family believes that our spiritual growth is important, so we attend church regularly and have a daily family devotional.
- There is a free flow of ideas in our family. Family members are encouraged and expected to express opinions and share ideas without fear of being put down, teased, or reprimanded.
- The ideas that family members share are judged on their merits rather than on their source. Even the youngest member of this family contributes good ideas.
- Rules and regulations do not define our family as much as our beliefs and values do.
- Our family shares authority and responsibility.
- Decisions in our family are made by those most capable of making them.

- Our family values learning and growing and recognizes that family members have the capacity to grow and change.
- Our family takes adequate time to discuss issues, reflect on them, and plan together.
- Cooperation is praised openly in our family.
- Thoughtful listening is modeled by parents and affirmed and appreciated by everyone.
- Volunteerism is a hallmark of the way we work together, and it is sincere.
- Our family has an openness to new ideas and the motivation to try them.
- Our family members appreciate and recognize the accomplishments of one another.
- Family members care for each other and have fun laughing together.
- We cultivate special traditions and celebrations in our family.
- We are honest and open in our communication. Everyone's opinion counts.

When you have constructed a vision statement, you will be ready to form a mission statement. The mission statement grows out of a family's vision, but it will be more practical than the vision statement. Since a mission statement is usually "measurable, obtainable, and purposeful," once the mission is achieved, a new one will be needed. Here's a portion of this family's mission statement:

- Our family will express its commitment to volunteerism by choosing a family volunteer project for the next six months.

- Our family will learn a new sport (like skiing, inline skating, or bowling) together during the next year.
- Our family will do a better job of recognizing the accomplishments of family members by using some of the activities listed in chapter 5.
- Our family will commit to a time of daily devotions.

Parents are responsible for the vision statement. Children and parents together are responsible for the mission statement. Everyone is responsible for making sure the mission is reached.

Perhaps the idea of developing vision and mission statements sounds rather lofty and impractical for you and your family. But let me challenge you: your children will grow up with or without a family mission and vision. Without a plan, it will happen willy-nilly. Why not have a plan before you begin that provides focus and direction?

## Your Children's Uniqueness

A second important component of developing your family team is intentionally determining and celebrating the uniqueness of each of your children. Children differ in temperament, personality, learning style, intelligence, gifts and talents, body type, birth order, and gender. They are complex and wonderful creatures. Parents must become skilled at discovering what Ralph Mattson and Thom Black call a child's "design."[1] You must uncover and build on the specific gifts that God has provided for your child. Chapter 3 will provide some in-depth discussion on the variety of ways that children can differ and ways to help you discover your child's unique gifts.

# Family Council

Another critical component of developing the family team is instituting a regular family meeting or family council. Family council is a concept advanced by Rudolf Dreikurs. Webster's defines a council as "an assembly of persons called together for consultation, deliberation, or discussion." Dreikurs describes the family council as a meeting where all family members can speak without interruption, with freedom of expression, without fear of recrimination, and without regard for age or status. Having a regularly scheduled family meeting means that the important task of family communication isn't left to chance. A regularly scheduled meeting gives everyone the feeling that there will be an opportunity to talk about problems, complaints, and suggestions in a forum where everyone else will listen. And that includes parents.

Our family came rather late to the idea of family council, and I well remember those times before we began to have them when I tried to broach the topic of family chores. At that point we had no mechanism for a family meeting, and no one had the time, inclination, or obligation to listen to my concerns (Dad included). Once the family council was instituted, everyone had a responsibility to listen to everyone else's concerns and to talk about them in the spirit of solving problems.

The family council operates under certain basic ground rules:

- Everyone who is living in the home constitutes the family council.
- The meetings are regularly scheduled. Nothing interferes with a family council meeting, and conversely, family council doesn't interfere with any other activities.
- Every family member gets to express his/her complaints, ideas, and opinions and must hear those of the others.
- Every family member gets a chance to speak, and for as long as he/she wants.
- Family members can speak without fear of consequences. No one is to be punished for something said during a family council.
- Everyone must be treated equally, regardless of age.
- When a decision is made it will only be binding if all the family members who are present agree to it.[2]

You may be shocked at the ground rules for a family council. You may feel they give children too much power in the family. But you will find if you implement the family council structure that family members will be happier, family life will be more efficient, communication will be opened up, and there will be less need for punishment.

Here's one parent's testimonial about the benefits her family derived from family councils.

My husband and I asked the children if they would be interested in trying a family council. The results have been as fascinating as they have been fantastic. We have all had to revamp our thinking and it has not been easy. We have had some setbacks that were learning experiences in themselves. There are six of us. My husband, Don, 31, is a carpenter; I'm 30, a housewife. Our children are Betty, 11½, sixth grade; Dick, 10; Janet, 7; and Roger, 6. We went into family councils rather hesitantly, with visions of each of our four children dictating to us. We were so wrong! We also had visions that this would be a big joke to them, and that they would really put us to a test to see how far we would go. We were wrong about that too.

At our first meeting we set a few ground rules, the biggest one being that this was not a gripe session. We started with what has always been the biggest bone of contention at our house: bedtime.

First we asked Betty what time she thought would be fair for her to retire, and to say why she thought so. She said ten o'clock because she is the oldest. Dick reminded us all that Betty never has to be called in the morning, that she always gets up by herself in plenty of time. The family voted, and she got the ten o'clock time. Dick was next. He said nine-thirty was a fine time for him, because Betty could then have the bathroom all to herself for a half hour. Janet was next, and said nine o'clock for her. Voted and passed. Then Roger said he'd like to stay up as late as Dick, but we disapproved. After discussion, we voted on eight-thirty, and he agreed.

By this time my husband and I were in a state of shock. We couldn't believe how serious our children were acting, and what good thinking they were using.

At this first historic meeting, we also discussed chores. I had always given each child mandatory chores each day, and watched until the chores got done. At the meeting, each child made a list of the chores he or she would agree to do for one week, and we discussed each list, changed some, and then agreed on them.

The first week was great. The children policed each other, and neither Don nor I had to say, "Go to bed" even once. We only had to remind anyone to do chores twice all week.

The second week wasn't quite as good, but we were all learning. At the second meeting, I brought up the problem of the children forgetting their lunches and told them that I would no longer bring them to school. Janet suggested that whoever forgot his or her lunch could charge lunch at school but would have to pay for it out of his or her own money. We all agreed.

At the third meeting we all opened up a bit more. I accused them of not living up their end of the deal, and they accused me of butting in too much. Don suggested it was time for more ground rules, and we agreed to have a chairman to preside at each meeting, rotating each week, so that each of us would have a regular turn to speak.

As we moved along from week to week, the time came when we reached a standstill and couldn't get agreement on the things that were bothering us. We suggested that we drop all agreements for a week and go back to the old ways to see how it would be. That whole week everybody was miserable. Don and I nagged, complained, hollered— everything we could think of and nobody liked it. When meeting time came around again Thursday night we started fresh, and I for one hope we never go through another week like that one.

Our whole family is learning to treat one another as equals, and I know if other families would try it, they would get as much out of it as we have.

Sincerely,
Madge Cooke[3]

Here are the steps for getting started if you want to try a family council at your house:

1. Set the date for the first meeting.
2. Invite everyone in the family to attend.
3. Include everyone who lives in the house (grandparents, exchange students, etc.)
4. Choose someone to preside over the meeting. Everyone should take a turn at being the facilitator (leader, chairperson), but it's best to have adults and older children fill this role at first so younger children can get the hang of it.
5. Give out information about what a family council is and how it works. If you don't know the answer, say so.
6. Figure out your ground rules.

7. Use parliamentary rules. Before someone speaks, he or she has to be recognized by the chairperson. No one can interrupt, correct, criticize, explain, or expand on anyone else's comments.
8. Don't devote the meeting exclusively to complaints.
9. Be prepared for making some wrong decisions. Sometimes parents will, in their superior wisdom, know that a decision is doomed for failure. But unless it's dangerous or life-threatening, let the decision stand. This is the way children will learn how to be responsible and accountable.
10. No one person is completely responsible for the functioning of the meeting. Everyone has an equal responsibility and share.

More specific how-to-do-it techniques for holding your own family council can be found in Dreikurs' book.

## Family Strategies and Activities

The final step in developing your family's teamwork system is to build in a variety of strategies and activities that manage sibling rivalry and build healthy relationships between your children. Strategies and activities are tools that can help facilitate good communication, decision making, problem solving, and team building. Parents don't always have to have the answers and solutions to every problem. Using an activity or process can help family members ask the right questions, discuss and debate ideas openly and freely, create a climate in the family conducive to discussing possible options, and reach quality decisions. Consult chapter 4 where you'll find many different strategies for handling sibling rivalry and building a family team. Then check out chapter 5 for a variety of activities to nurture supportive siblings. Begin to practice and integrate these strategies and activities into your family life as needed, and you will be amazed at the spirit of teamwork and sibling cooperation that will begin to emerge.

## Endnotes

1. Ralph Mattson and Thom Black, *Discovering Your Child's Design* (Elgin, Ill.: Cook Publishing, 1989).

2. Rudolf Dreikurs, Shirley Gould, and Raymond J. Corsini, *Family Council: The Dreikurs' Technique for Putting an End to War between Parents and Children (and between Children and Children)* (Chicago: Henry Regnery Company, 1974), pp. 12-14.

3. Ibid., pp. 20-21.

# 3

# Understanding Your Child's Uniqueness

**T**here's only one sure-fire way to reduce, if not eliminate sibling rivalry, and that's to love, appreciate, and affirm each child's unique qualities. The child who feels disadvantaged and self-respect is far more likely to feel jealous and hostile toward his/her siblings. But affirming uniqueness and appreciating differences is a difficult thing to do in a society whose constitutional foundations are based on the principle of equality. Trying to treat your children as equals, however, rather than as unique individuals will make you a crazy person and result in children who spend their lives adding up the parental ledger constantly looking for shortfalls.

There are so many different ways and dimensions in which to understand and appreciate your child; you may not be able to cover them all. But be eclectic in your approach, and enjoy the process. Each psychologist or child development specialist has a personal model for explaining why people (children) behave the way they do. These professionals have devoted their lives' work to coming up with one sure-fire way of categorizing and defining people. They then work to make all behavior fit into those categories. Kevin Leman can explain all of our behavior based on our birth order. Thomas Armstrong tells us we need to pay attention to learning styles. And Harvard psychologist Howard Gardner categorizes everybody according to one of seven multiple intelligences. Take your pick, but don't focus on only one dimension. The important thing is to become aware of the unique qualities of each of your children, to appreciate and affirm them, and then to help siblings do the same for each other.

Before we talk about all of the different ways you can begin to get to know your children, I want to introduce you to a wonderful book entitled *Born to Fly*.[1] The author, Thom Black, advises parents to systematically set about making observations and gathering evidence about their children to better understand and appreciate each child's uniqueness. The basic areas he lists include many of the categories mentioned above: how your child relates to people (personality); in what way your child learns (learning styles); what excites and interests each child (intelligences); and what kind of discipline each child needs (temperament). Once you've figured out each of your children's unique attributes, you won't ever again be tempted to treat them equally.

As you read the following material, jot down ideas and descriptions of your child as they occur to you. Of course, the younger your children, the more challenging will be your task.

# Learning Styles

Knowing how your child learns best is helpful information as he or she begins school, but this understanding can also help as you interact and work with your child at home.

**Visual/auditory/kinesthetic learners.** Let's use an example to help you understand these styles. Suppose that someone told you your life depended on mastering seven principles of survival in the wilderness. At the end of the course, you will be sent into the wilderness to survive. The choice of how you want to learn the seven principles is up to you. Would you prefer a lecture the subject? Then you're probably an auditory learner. Perhaps you'd rather read a textbook? Visual learners need to see what they have to learn in print or in pictures. Or would you choose to have an expert demonstrate each principle and then let you experience them for yourself in a game or simulation? Then you're a kinesthetic learner. You like hands-on experiences and learning by doing.

I personally would like to read the material first, then attend the lecture, and finally try out what I've learned in the real world. But there are many who would move to the hands-on experience at the outset and never need to read or hear about what they need to do. The efficient learner has a well-developed repertoire of learning styles. But many children can only learn new concepts and skills if they are presented in their primary learning style.

If your child has always loved to sit still and listen to stories, then chances are that child is an auditory learner. He or she can probably understand and remember material better if it is heard. The visual learner, on the other hand, needs to see something written down or illustrated before he or she can remember it. If your child has to touch everything in sight, take it apart and see how it works, then chances are that the kinesthetic mode is your child's preferred learning style. This particular way of looking at learning styles is the most simplistic. It simply looks at the preferred method of taking information into the brain. Understanding this information may, however, give you insight into why one of your children is always taking things apart and asking questions and another one is perfectly content to sit quietly reading a book. Both have admirable and unique qualities. They're just different.

There are many different ways of describing learning styles, almost as many ways as there are theorists who have studied the subject. The theorists apply different labels to the same generic characteristics and knowing just which labels which theorists use is not particularly important. What *is* important is to have an understanding of your child's strengths and weaknesses and how he or she learns best. Looking at this idea in a variety of ways will help you construct the most complete picture you can of your child.

**Brain hemispheres.** Another, more complex approach to learning styles originated with the discovery that the brain is divided into two sections or hemispheres. Researchers discovered in working with "split-brain" patients, those who had the major connection between the brain hemispheres cut due to severe epilepsy, that certain behaviors and ways of thinking seemed to be centered in one hemisphere or the other. Of course, unless our hemispheres have been disconnected, we all use both. But many individuals show a definite preference for either the right or left side; thus the labels "right-brained" and "left-brained."

Distinctly right-brained individuals make better artists and performers. Distinctly left-brained people do better as accountants or chemists. We survived for centuries without knowing about hemisphericity, but an understanding of which thinking or reasoning patterns (learning styles) characterize each hemisphere, along with the related school skills, can be helpful for the parent. This approach to looking at learning styles focuses on what the learner actually does with the information in his brain, once he has successfully learned it either visually, auditorially, or kinesthetically.

Primarily left-brained individuals do their processing (thinking, reasoning) in an *analytical-sequential* fashion. They prefer verbal explanations, use language to remember, produce ideas logically, like structured experiences, and approach problems seriously.[2] The school skills that relate to this type of processing are symbols, language, reading, phonics, locating details and facts, talking and reciting, following directions, listening, and auditory association.[3] Needless to say, they like school.

Individuals who are primarily right-brained do their processing in a *wholistic-simultaneous* way. They prefer visual explanations, use images to remember, produce ideas intuitively, prefer abstract thinking tasks, like open-ended and fluid experiences, and approach problems playfully.[4] The school skills that relate to this type of processing are spatial relationships, mathematical concepts, color sensitivity, singing and music, art expression, creativity, and visualization.[5] The challenge faced by parents of strongly right-brained children is in finding school settings and teachers that tap into the learning strengths of their children.

**Temperaments and learning patterns.** Thus far we've looked at learning styles from the standpoint of how information is taken in by the learner (auditory, visual, kinesthetic) and ways in which information is processed by different sides of the brain. A third way of looking at learning styles integrates the child's temperament with his style of learning, which adds another dimension to our understanding. Dr. Keith Golay has developed a different way of looking at your child's learning patterns and temperaments.[6] He suggests four categories: *actual-spontaneous, actual-routine, conceptual-specific,* and *conceptual-global.*

Children who are described as *actual-spontaneous* are hands-on, active learners. They don't have time to go through the planning and organizing stages of a project. They want to jump right in and do it. They want things to move quickly and be active. Art, music, and physical education are their favorite subjects. They hate homework and can't stand anyone telling them what to do. The actual-spontaneous learner despises the structure of school and can't wait to get out of the classroom. He needs tasks that involve manipulating, constructing, and operating to be truly fulfilled.

*Actual-routine* children are perfect students. Their desks are well organized. They love the systems of school: the rules, the routine, the memorization and drill. They have to be forced to break out of their molds to try creative writing, drama, or role playing. Just give the actual-routine child a workbook and he or she will be happy all day. The actual-routine child loves helping the teacher and can be found after school emptying wastebaskets or cleaning the blackboard.

The third type of learner is *conceptual-specific*. These children aren't as social as they probably should be. They get impatient when other people don't understand as quickly as they do. They like math, science, engineering, and problem solving. They find group discussions a waste of time and resent the constant repetition of previously mastered material. They have an insatiable desire to learn and pick up information in an effortless way. They are frequently seen by their peers as "different." Unless guided toward appropriate social graces, the conceptual-specific child can become an isolate.

The fourth and final category, *conceptual-global,* contains children who do well in school but thrive on cooperation rather than competition. These children prefer the humanities rather than the sciences and enjoy group discussions, role playing, and the good feeling that comes from making a contribution to a group. The conceptual-global child is a "people person" and seems to have an innate sense of how to get along with others. Friends frequently seek this child out for assistance and advice.

**The 4Mat system.** A final way in which to look at learning styles is to focus on the specific types of school activities and teaching styles that meet the needs of the various learning styles. Bernice McCarthy, author of the 4Mat system, suggests another way of looking at learning styles and warns of the problems that can occur when a teacher or parent has a dramatically different learning style from the child. McCarthy has developed four style categories: *innovative, analytic, common sense,* and *dynamic.*[7]

*Innovative* children learn by listening to others and sharing ideas. They start with what they see and then generalize. They enjoy small-group interaction, role playing, team sports, and simulation, but they don't like timed tests, debates, and computer-assisted instruction. They want to know how things directly affect the lives of those around them.

*Analytic* learners enjoy listening to the teacher lecture. They are thinkers and watchers with rational and sequential thinking patterns. They enjoy programmed instruction, well-organized lectures or stories, competition, demonstration, and objective tests, but dislike role play, open discussion, and group projects. They want realistic and practical information and tend to be perfectionistic.

Students with the *common sense* style enjoy problem solving, debates, logic problems, independent study, and especially experiments that build on what they have learned. They do not value input while they are trying things out. They dislike memorizing, a lot of reading, group work, and writing assignments. They need to be challenged to check the validity of their knowledge. They want to discover how things work and how they can be applied to real life. They may be mislabeled as "hyperactive" but will respond to a teacher who is an intellectual challenger and fellow learner and who is logical and just.

*Dynamic* children like to see, hear, touch, and feel. They get bored easily unless they can learn by trial and error, taking action, and carrying out plans. They enjoy case studies, guided imagery, drama, creative productions, and assignments that require originality. They dislike assignments without options, standard routines, or activities done in haste. They want a teacher who is a facilitator and stimulator of ideas and who is curious and imaginative, encouraging them to explore the possibilities of what there is to know.

Do you recognize any of your children's qualities yet? If not, try this approach to understanding why children behave the way they do.

## Intelligences

David Wechsler, developer of a widely used intelligence test, defined intelligence as "the global capacity of an individual to act purposefully, to think rationally, and to deal effectively with his environment." But there are many who caution against such a narrow view. Defining intelligence strictly on the basis of one test does a disservice to the many kinds of gifts and talents that cannot be measured by a test alone.

Howard Gardner, a Harvard psychologist, hypothesizes seven kinds of intelligence located in different parts of the brain: *linguistic, logical-mathematical, spatial, musical, bodily kinesthetic, interpersonal,* and *intrapersonal.* His ideas are fascinating and give us one more way to look at how to encourage the gifts and talents of our children.[8]

*Linguistic* intelligence is centered in language. Readers, writers, storytellers are all linguistically gifted. Children with these gifts like to write, read, spell, do crossword puzzles, and play word games. (But all children should do these things as part of their growing-up experience—not just those who seem to gravitate in that direction.)

Individuals with *logical-mathematical* intelligence think conceptually. They love figuring out the answers to difficult problems and most likely are very logical thinkers. Children with strengths in this area like computers, chess, checkers, strategy games, and puzzles.

*Spatially* intelligent people think in images and pictures. They can draw, design, and visualize the way a room will look with new furniture and wallpaper. Children with strengths in this area spend a lot of time in art-related activities.

*Musical* intelligence and *bodily kinesthetic* intelligence relate to expertise in the areas of performing and composing music, and sports and physical activities, respectively.

The last two areas are the most fascinating to me since they hypothesize two areas that we frequently overlook when talking about intelligence: *interpersonal* and *intrapersonal* skills. The interpersonal people understand others. They are the leaders and communicators. The salesman that sold you the car you didn't think you needed probably had a high level of interpersonal intelligence.

*Intrapersonal* intelligence is just the opposite. Individuals with this quality are very independent. They rely on their own judgment, have a deep sense of self-confidence, and generally don't care what everyone else is wearing or doing. They have their own agenda.

## Temperament

The area of children's temperaments has been an especially interesting one for psychologists. Stella Chess and Alexander Thomas are the most well known.[9] They suggest eight different temperamental attributes of infants that generally follow a child into maturity: *activity level, rhythmicity, approach or withdrawal, adaptability, sensory threshold, quality of mood and intensity of expressiveness, distractibility,* and *persistence and attention span.* Here's a brief general description of each, along with some personal examples describing one of my own children, Emily, now twenty-five and in graduate school.

**Activity level** is the amount of movement and motion engaged in by an infant or child. Some children do everything at top speed, and others need plenty of time to accomplish their tasks. While I am generally in the "fast forward" mode, my daughter Emily moves at a much slower pace, particularly when she eats. When we go out for lunch or dinner, I always leave extra time. Instead of complaining, I've learned to appreciate the way she enjoys her food and conversation at mealtimes.

**Rhythmicity or regularity** describes how readily a child adapts to a schedule and routine. Irregular children eat, sleep, and toilet train in unusual and unpredictable ways. Despite the best efforts of their parents, they operate on their own timetable. My daughter Emily fought sleeping through the night. She fought being toilet trained. As a young adult she has adapted to many different time zones and work schedules, a credit to her maturity and adaptability.

**Approach or withdrawal** describes the way in which infants and children react to new experiences. New playmates, nursery school, kindergarten, the first year of college—each new experience calls for an adjustment. The child who responds positively to new situations makes life easier for parents. Life was never that easy for Emily. She needed time to warm up, opportunities to feel comfortable and fit in, and patient understanding from her parents. Once she warmed up, she was always a star, but we needed to help her get over the initial "hump" and know that better times were ahead.

**Adaptability** has to do with the ways an infant or child reacts to change. Low adaptability and withdrawal frequently go together. Although adaptability is certainly a plus in a very young child, when considered in the light of peer pressure and susceptibility to being swayed, the quality becomes less attractive. Emily is never easily swayed. She has always been able to maintain her own personhood and define her own views. As a young adult she is a very independent person.

**Sensory threshold** describes the level of sensitivity to nuances of color, music, texture, and light. I describe this characteristic as "the princess and the pea syndrome." Children with a low sensory threshold are more easily awakened by light and noise, are fussier about the clothes they wear, and would like to redecorate their room almost as soon as they are aware that their taste differs substantially from their parents. Emily started redecorating her room with magic markers at the age of three. It was too dull, she informed me.

**Quality of mood and intensity of expressiveness** describes the way in which a child reacts to life's situations. Does the child react with delight, enthusiasm, and expressiveness at positive happenings? Or is he or she more taciturn and silent? Emily has always been talkative, expressive, and enthusiastic—unless she happens to disagree wholeheartedly with your position. Then she digs her heels in and states her case. I still enjoy hearing all the details of her graduate school experiences—which she relates with zest and humor.

**Distractibility** is another quality of temperament, which has to do with how easily a child or infant can be taken off task by something else in the environment. "The house could be burning around her and she wouldn't notice it." This ability to concentrate and focus on things has been a real asset to Emily in her academic career.

**Persistence and attention span** are qualities related to distractibility. Although persistence can drive you crazy in a small child, once this same child begins school, persistence will be a valued commodity. Again, Emily was at the outside edge of the continuum. Her persistence often made her somewhat inflexible, but that quality has helped her accomplish a multitude of personal and academic goals.

Emily's father and I recognized her problems and limitations, guided, advised, and set limits where needed, and affirmed and encouraged the gifts and strengths of our daughter. Is she perfect? Of course not. Is she unique? You bet! Does she know that? If she doesn't already, she certainly will when she finishes reading this book!

But the most important question for you is this: What are *you* going to do with all of this information when *you* finish reading this book? My suggestions are these:

- Find out what your child shines in. It could be music, sports, getting along with people, caring for others, or any one of a thousand gifts and talents.
- Accept your child's gifts even if they are not abilities that you particularly prize. I certainly hope you're not trying to make your child into a Heisman trophy winner if he can't throw a football—or already programming her to be a doctor when you don't have a sense of her abilities in science or math.
- Draw out your child's gifts, but don't pressure him to develop them. Just because your child is good at something doesn't mean he'll want to pursue it. Emily was a talented French horn player. Her teacher said she had great promise, but she didn't want to devote her time and energies to that pursuit. She wanted to draw, design, and write. We can nurture, but we can't mandate!

**Endnotes**

1. Thom Black, with Lynda Stephenson, *Born to Fly* (Grand Rapids, Mich.: Zondervan, 1994).

2. James T. Webb, Elizabeth A. Meckstroth, and Stephanie Tolan, *Guiding the Gifted Child* (Columbus: Ohio Psychology Publishing, 1982), p. 52.

3. Barbara Meister Vitale, *Unicorns Are Real: A Right Brained Approach to Learning* (Rolling Hills Estate, Calif.: Jalmar Press, 1982), p. 9.

4. Webb, p. 52.

5. Vitale, p. 9.

6. Keith Golay, *Learning Patterns and Temperament Styles* (Fullerton, Calif.: Manas-Systems, 1982), pp. 27-44.

7. Bernice McCarthy and Susan Leflar, eds., *4Mat in Action: Creative Lesson Plans for Teaching to Learning Styles with Right/Left Mode Techniques* (Barrington, Ill.: Excel, 1983).

8. Howard Gardner, *Frames of Mind: The Theory of Multiple Intelligences* (New York: Basic Books, 1983).

9. Stella Chess and Alexander Thomas, *Know Your Child: An Authoritative Guide for Today's Parents* (New York: Basic Books, 1987).

# 4

# Strategies for Building a Family Team

**Y**ou probably won't be able to totally eliminate sibling rivalry from your household scene, but here are strategies for reducing sibling rivalry and making life more peaceable. Choose the ones that meet your needs and practice using them with your children. Even if they don't work perfectly the first time, try them again. I often became frustrated when reading about a new method or approach to discipline or parenting and wished that someone had encouraged me to be a little more persistent. If at first you don't succeed, give it another try. And don't be afraid to add your own creative twists to the strategies.

## Strategy #1: Acknowledge a child's feelings.

Instead of insisting that your child dismiss negative feelings about a sibling, acknowledge the existence of

51

those feelings and encourage discussion. I personally need to exercise discipline when my children are verbally venting to or about their brother or sister. My first reaction is often to argue or defend the other sibling or in some cases to completely agree. But instead, I discipline myself to listen, acknowledge, and restate. If you are acknowledging feelings with a younger child, you may need to help that child put his or her feelings into words. But avoid being judgmental. It's not your responsibility to hand your child a solution on a silver platter. Don't fall into the "wise and all-knowing" parent trap either. Lecturing, pontificating, and moralizing are no-no's. Be an active listener, maintaining eye contact. You will discover, as I have, that insisting upon good feelings between children (which are in reality false and pretentious) *can* lead to bad feelings. And amazingly enough, allowing for bad feelings between children can eventually lead to good feelings.

## Strategy #2: Confront wishful thinking.

Children will sometimes give voice to horrible wishes about their siblings like "I hate him," "I wish he were dead," or "Why doesn't he just leave home?" Our first reaction is to argue with the child: "You don't hate your brother." Another common reaction is to berate the child for his feelings and make him feel even worse: "That's a terrible thing to say."

A better way is to help children work through their feelings and even startle them into actually thinking about what they've said by giving them in fantasy what they can never have in reality. Making statements such as, "Oh, you'd like to get rid of your brother," or "You think it would be much nicer around here if your brother moved out," may seem outrageous, but when you verbalize the thought, the angry child who made it will usually realize the enormity of his statement and calm down. Some particularly insightful or sophisticated children, as well as adults, will become annoyed with a restatement of their feelings. For those individuals, use responses like "Tell me more about it," or "Explain what you mean by that."

## Strategy #3: Put it in writing.

Help your children channel their hostile feeling into symbolic or creative acts like drawing a picture, telling a story using dolls or toy figures, or writing a story. One child I knew published her own book when she was in fourth grade. Titled "101 Ways to Bug Your Brother," it contained a catalog of the plagues she planned to systematically visit on her brother, exacting revenge for all of the hateful things he'd done to her. Now grown, she and her brother can laugh at her creation, but at the time, writing it all down was a productive way of dealing with her feelings.

## Strategy #4: Do as I do (and also as I say).

I sometimes feel like a broken record when I write books for parents as I remind them to model the traits and characteristics that they desire in their children. You will rarely find children rising above the level of their parents' behavior. If you want your children to be polite, respectful, and considerate, "walk your talk."

## Strategy #5: Re-place your attention.

Our first inclination when forced to deal with a problem occurring between two or more siblings is to give our immediate attention to the person "dishing out the dirt." Disciplining the guilty party or removing the aggressor from the fracas satisfies our need for immediate justice, but it gives the perpetrator just what he wants, our attention. Instead, try giving your attention to the injured party, ignoring the troublemaker. Re-placing your attention will often modify the troublemaker's behavior when he figures out that misbehaving is not the way to get his share of your time.

## Strategy #6: Accentuate the positive.

Increase the number of positive child-parent interactions. When kids are behaving we ignore them. The minute they act up, we zoom in with both barrels blazing. The first focus of your behavior management plan will be to become aware of, adept in, and focused on using "differential attention." This means that you're going to work at "catching your child being good" and at those moments give positive attention. There is, however, something deeply ingrained in our psyche that seems to believe it's better to "let well enough alone." The average parent thinks to herself, *Next thing you know, she'll be wanting my attention all the time.* But it just doesn't work that way.

Miraculously enough, once you show an interest in your child and approach her rather than waiting to be "asked" for attention, the quality of your relationship and time spent together will deepen. There are several ways to have this positive interaction, depending on the situation and the age of the child. One way is to simply provide a commentary or description of what your child is doing. Don't lecture or teach. Simply observe and comment (e.g., "That's a really interesting bridge you're building"). Comment only on positive things the child is doing. A second way of building positive interactions is by rewarding your child. These "rewards" come in the form of physical affection such a hug, kiss, or pat; a praise statement that is general in nature (e.g., "Very nice work"); or a specific praise statement that describes a very particular behavior that you are reinforcing (e.g., "Thank you for sharing your toys with Susie").

Here are several rules that are worth mentioning for using praise with children.[1]

**Praise behavior, not personality.** Take care to avoid using words like *good* and *bad*. Rather, describe the specific actions that are eliciting your praise.

**Use specific praise.** There's nothing worse than empty praise. "You've done a great job" doesn't motivate and inform me like "You really made me feel a part of the group during that discussion."

**Praise progress.** Communicate the concept of lifelong learning to your child. We're never there! We are always growing and changing. Point out the difference between his behavior/achievement today in comparison to last week or last month.

**Praise appropriately.** Don't overdo praise in public for shy children. And, don't praise a child to the skies for a tiny accomplishment. Design the praise to fit the milestone.

**Give praise immediately.** Don't save it up for a rainy day. Deliver that compliment on the spot.

**Mix praise with unconditional love.** While praise is important, don't ever send the message to your child that your love is conditional upon achievement and accomplishment. Be there with love no matter what!

## Strategy #7: Reward good behavior.

Using specific tangible reinforcement procedures to increase positive behaviors works well when you're trying to change unacceptable behavior patterns like sibling fighting and name-calling. As an elementary school principal I frequently inherited the behavior problems that were hard-core. The teacher and parent had tried everything and nothing worked. My favorite was Dylan. A fourth grader, he simply didn't do his work. Not only did he not turn in any homework assignments, he just didn't bother to work much during the school day either. Dylan was obviously starved for attention. And he'd been getting plenty of it. The teacher was "on his case" from morn till dusk. And then his mother took over from there.

I spent some time talking with Dylan and found out what his favorite restaurant was. It just happened to be mine as well. We both had an obsession with cheeseburgers and french fries from McDonald's. I didn't have a clue as to whether my plan would work, but since all else had failed, I had nothing to lose. Dylan needed immediate feedback, but my budget and schedule did not permit daily lunches at the Golden Arches. So I proposed to Dylan that if he could complete all of his assignments for three consecutive days, on the fourth day, I would take him to lunch at McDonald's. He brightened at the prospect. But I'd been fooled before. I checked in at the end of the first day. Dylan was on track. Ditto for day two. I held my breath for day three, but Dylan came through for me. Dylan and I became good friends as he moved through fifth and sixth grade.

Our lunches became more infrequent, but I never stopped going to lunch with him. I discovered many of the challenges that faced him in his home life, and he got to know all about my children and work. I've tried this same system on other students, and it doesn't always work. They didn't find the idea of a one-on-one lunch with an adult all that attractive. To design a reward system that works for you, you'll need to determine what your child's preferences may be at any given time. And then be prepared to vary the menu of choices as time passes. Of course, your budget and family values must always be kept in the forefront as you determine what reinforcers will be used. And eventually you'll want the positive behaviors to become habit forming and you'll withdraw the tangible rewards.

## Strategy #8: Ignore bad behavior.

Use ignoring to decrease negative behaviors. Logic tells us that this statement makes sense, but it's much easier said than done. Most parents try ignoring and then report that it doesn't work. But perhaps you haven't "really" ignored your child. Here are some very specific things you need to do when you ignore.

**No eye contact or nonverbal cues.** Deliberately turn your body away so that if you inadvertently smile or frown, your response cannot be noted by your child.

**No verbal contact.** Don't give any explanations or rationales for your behavior. Don't respond to your child when she asks why you are ignoring. If you feel the need to explain anything to your child, do it well before using the technique, and use statements such as "I'm going to ignore you when you're doing _____, and when you stop, I will stop ignoring you." You can then demonstrate the ignoring technique to your child.

## Strategy #9: Give clear instructions.

Some parents spray commands at their children like machine-gun bullets, hoping that one or more will find a mark, but are unprepared to follow up if their directives are ignored. There are several other inappropriate ways to give commands that cause confusion and noncompliance from children. Chaining together several unrelated commands will cause an information overload and virtually assure that nothing will happen. A typical chain command is, "Turn off the TV; put away your toys; and finish your homework." Vague and ambiguous commands are often ignored as well. "Be nice to your brother" is a perfect example of a vague command. While Mom may know perfectly well what the definition of "nice" is (no name-calling, no physical contact, and positive conversation), she has not communicated that concept to the child at all.

My favorite type of command that is sure to be ignored is the oxymoronic "question command." "Would you like to have dinner now?" The parent is well-meaning and feels he/she is being polite, but to the child there is clearly a choice involved. And odds are, the reply will be "no." Requests in and of themselves are OK, but make sure you don't use the request format when what you really want is immediate compliance.

When commands are phrased in the "Let's _____" mode, you are sending the message that you will be involved in the activity (e.g., "Let's pick up your toys"). If you don't intend to share the responsibility, then don't use those words. Your child may feel tricked and used. He has a genuine excuse for noncompliance if you don't help.

Many parents feel compelled to give lengthy explanations and rationales in conjunction with their commands. If you must give an explanation, then give it first, before you give the command. The last thing your child hears should be the clear and explicit directive. All other words will be lost.

Here are a few simple rules for giving appropriate commands.

**Be specific and direct.** Make sure you have your child's attention, and establish eye contact.

**Give only one command at a time.**

**Wait five seconds** for compliance before giving any additional instructions.

## Strategy #10: Use negative consequences.

Rely on consequences to decrease inappropriate behaviors. Some authors use the word *punishment* to describe what happens when a child misbehaves. I prefer the phrase "negative consequences." If your child doesn't perceive the consequences as negative, then they won't be successful in decreasing the inappropriate behavior. Some children delight in being sent to their rooms. They have TVs, VCRs, computers, and hand-held video games. Where's the punishment? In order for negative consequences to be effective, remember to apply these helpful rules:

■ Make sure that both you and your child know exactly what the target behavior is that you are trying to eliminate (e.g., interrupting, fighting with sister, talking back to parent).

■ Make sure that the consequence follows immediately on the heels of the offending behavior.

■ Make sure that the consequence follows after each and every occurrence of the offending behavior.

■ Make sure that you are calm and matter-of-fact when you administer the consequence. If your child suspects for a moment that you are frenzied and frantic, kiss compliance good-bye.

■ Make sure that when your child exhibits the desired behavior he is positively reinforced.

## Strategy #11: Overcorrect to diminish inappropriate behaviors.

Overcorrection was first suggested by Dr. Nathan Azrin, a psychologist, and consists of having a child practice and practice and practice the "right" way to behave or do a task. The consequence of repetition is designed to eradicate the unwanted behavior. I've used this procedure with great success on students who persisted in running in the halls. After they practiced "running" up and down the halls (with parental permission, of course) for thirty minutes after school, they were more inclined to think twice before racing headlong toward the gymnasium or washrooms when with their classmates.

## Strategy #12: Use a token system.

The most common behavioral management systems involve some kind of token economy based on points, or an object of some sort (some families use poker chips, but if you find this objectionable, find another kind of token in the toy or hobby shop). The token economy system is very similar to the monetary system on which our society operates, only much smaller in scale. Children will earn tokens or points for their "work," which is actually compliance with rules. They will then be able to exchange their tokens or points for a variety of rewards. Use of the token economy with children younger than three is not practical, since their ability to comprehend symbols and numbers is not at an appropriate developmental level.

There are a number of accepted and well researched advantages to a token economy program.

- Token systems permit parents to manage child behavior by drawing on rewards that are more powerful than mere praise and attention. Hence, you can often achieve greater and more rapid improvements in compliance, beyond what attention could accomplish.
- Token systems are highly convenient reward systems. Chips and points can be taken anywhere, dispensed anywhere and anytime, and used to earn virtually any form of privilege or tangible incentive.
- Token rewards are likely to retain their value or effectiveness throughout the day across numerous situations. In contrast, children often satiate quickly with food rewards, stickers, or other tangible reinforcers. Because tokens can be exchanged for an almost limitless variety of rewards, their effectiveness as reinforcers is less likely to fluctuate than that of a particular reward, such as food or stickers.
- Token systems permit a more organized, systematic, and fair approach to managing children's behavior. The system makes it very clear what children earn for particular behaviors and how many points or chips are required for access to each privilege or reward. This precludes the arbitrariness often seen in typical parent management approaches where

a child may be granted a reward or privilege on the spur of the moment because the parent is in a good mood rather than because the child has earned it. Similarly, it prevents parents from denying earned rewards simply because the child misbehaved once during the day.

■ Token systems result in increased parental attention to appropriate child behavior and compliance. Because parents must dispense the tokens, they must attend and respond more often to child behaviors they might otherwise have overlooked. The children also make parents more aware of their successes or accomplishments so as to earn the tokens.

■ Token systems teach a fundamental concept of society: privileges and rewards as well as most of the things we desire in life must be earned by the way we behave. This is the work ethic that parents naturally wish to instill in their children: the harder they work and the more they apply themselves to handling responsibilities, the greater will be the rewards they receive.

## Strategy #13: Give time-outs.

Time-out is a very effective disciplinary tool. Used properly it means removing a child from a situation that is enjoyable and full of positive reinforcement to a much less pleasant situation. Time-out is a wonderful alternative to spanking younger children and an excellent way to remove an older child from a potentially explosive situation. There are several important rules to remember.

**The time-out location** must be safe (in case your child becomes upset or agitated), uninteresting, and away from mainstream activity. The child must desperately prefer to be anywhere else but in the time-out location.

**The time-out rules** must be carefully explained to your child ahead of time. Be sure to tell your child that every time he/she engages in a certain behavior, a time-out will result. If your child refrains from that behavior, no time-out will occur.

**Set a reasonable time limit** for the time-out based on the child's age. One minute per year of age is reasonable. If your child resists, add minutes for noncompliance. Lead your child back to the time-out area, but do not exceed more than three one-minute add-ons. You'll probably need to try another consequence if the penalties don't work.

**Brief periods of grounding** function as "time-out" for older children (over 12), but beware of anything longer than a few days.

**Never apologize for or discuss** the time-out after it's over. And don't require your child to apologize for being in time-out. Once the time-out is over, repeat your command if you were asking your child to do something. Be consistent and mean business.

**Catch your child being good** as soon as possible after a time-out, and give him some praise. This will let him know that you aren't holding a grudge and that you will always give him positive attention when he behaves appropriately.

# Strategy #14: Use active listening.

Effective and active listening is a very important part of solving sibling rivalry problems. Here are some important principles to keep in mind when you want "real" communication to take place between you and your children.

**Listen to the content.** Make sure you heard the words and ideas that the child is conveying to you.

**Listen to the intent.** Try to "hear between the lines." The emotional tone, pitch, and pace will often tell you more about what is being said than the actual words.

**Be alert for nonverbal language.** We often call this "body language." Gestures, facial expressions, and posture communicate just as powerfully as words.

**Pay attention to your nonverbal language.** If you're fidgeting or frowning you could be communicating a lack of interest or hostility toward what your child is saying to you.

**Try to be empathetic and nonjudgmental.** You can do this by trying to put yourself in another's position.

# Strategy #15: Resolve conflicts.

Thomas Gordon suggests three basic ways for resolving conflict in your family: modifying the environment, changing your behavior, and problem solving with children.[2]

**Modifying the environment** can be done in several ways. *Enriching* the environment gives children more stimuli, more opportunities for creativity, and reduces boredom which can often cause conflict. *Impoverishing* the environment means removing stimuli and calming children down (e.g., turning off the television, putting all the toys away, quietly sitting on the edge of the bed talking). *Restricting* the environment means that certain types of activities and play are confined to certain areas (e.g., roughhouse play only takes place in the basement or out-of-doors). *Child-proofing* the environment means removing all the sources of potential conflict or danger. *Planning ahead* means letting children know in advance about changes or helping them get things done before deadlines.

**Changing ourselves** is not an avenue of action that we generally consider when we want our children to improve their behavior, but I speak from experience when I tell you that it is a powerful tool. You can do this in a number of ways: (1) *Educate* yourself about child development. Attend parenting classes, consult with friends, or read a book. Broadening our knowledge base will frequently give us the perspective we need to approach conflict with more confidence. (2) *Have fun with your kids.* Add pleasurable memories to the bank, and they will carry you through the dark days of conflict. (3) *Make time for your own wants and needs.* Being good to yourself will enable you to approach conflict in a positive way. Go out for lunch or dinner. Have a massage. Take a vacation with just your spouse.

**Structured problem solving.** Use a structured method for resolving conflict in your family. Here's a model that we've used in our family. When I was a single parent, I sometimes took my older children out to a restaurant to engage in conflict resolution. They were on their best behavior in a neutral setting and this often served to bring a measure of calm to a potentially explosive situation. I've also used this model to resolve arguments between students in my school.

- Call a meeting of the concerned parties and explain the purpose of the meeting.
- Explain the ground rules to everyone.
- Write down each child's feelings and concerns. Read them aloud to both children to be sure you've understood them correctly.
- Allow each child time for rebuttal.
- Invite everyone to suggest as many solutions as possible.
- Write down all ideas without evaluating. Don't skip this part of the process. Seeing their ideas written down will help defuse angry feelings and also help children see the ideas more objectively.
- Decide upon the solutions you can all live with.

## Strategy #16: Keep a diary.

You will often be able to pinpoint exactly which situations bring out the worst episodes of sibling rivalry as well as when they occur by keeping a log of your children's behavior. One family discovered that the worst time for family fights was just before bedtime. Another peak time occurred before breakfast.

The bathroom was a frequent source of argument and irritation, so the next family meeting focused on brainstorming some solutions to the "bathroom problem."

## Strategy #17: Negotiate.

Kids should not only know what negotiation is and how to define it, they should have some modeling at home as to how it works so they can do it with their siblings. This gives them an alternative to fighting. In order to be a good negotiator, one must be able to imagine alternatives. This is a sophisticated skill that will have to be taught over time. Model give-and-take for your children. Demonstrate the art of reciprocal trading. Help your children think ahead to the logical consequences of their behavior.

## Strategy #18: Separate the siblings.

It's amazing how a little distance between siblings can ameliorate potentially explosive situations. When siblings are having problems, send them to separate rooms, enroll them in different programs, put them on different schedules, or encourage them to play different instruments. Put one in the front seat and one in the back if you can. When you know that two personalities don't mix well, plan ahead for seating in church, movies, and long vacations.

## Strategy #19: Write out a contract.

A contract is a formal document, much like a business contract, that spells out very clearly certain behavioral standards and expectations to which all family members will adhere. The contract also spells out the consequences for noncompliance. I frequently used contracts with students in my classroom as a teacher and in my school as a principal. Everyone who must abide by the contract should have input into its construction. Contracts that are drawn up by parents and imposed on the children will never work as well as those that are developed jointly. Just as in a business contract, everyone signs the contract. Make sure that the contract is not too complicated. It should define only one specific situation or behavior. For example: "The following individuals agree that they will not borrow anything that does not belong to them without first asking the permission of the owner." Beware of making contracts with children, however, if you feel that democracy and joint decision making don't have a place in the family setting. You'll be setting yourself up for disappointment and failure.

## Strategy #20: Be generous with "warm fuzzies."

Warm fuzzies are compliments and affirming statements that are made to fellow family members. Fighting, name-calling, and cutting remarks are the foundation of sibling rivalry. And some siblings know exactly how to zero in on each other's weak spots (e.g., clumsiness, stupidity, big ears). Take time during the dinner hour or a family meeting to write two warm fuzzies about each family member.

## Strategy #21: Share and share alike.

Parents can't make sharing happen by the sheer force of their will and moral standards. When parents are the ones who decide what gets shared and for how long, children usually end up becoming more dependent upon their parents and more resentful of their siblings. When we are forced to share, we clutch our belongings to us more tightly. A sharing atmosphere will begin to blossom when children have rights to their own things and are permitted to make their own decisions to share. So, never force your children to share. Make a point of sharing yourself and praise those children in your family who do. William Damon[3] points out the most common sources of children's sharing:

- the child's initial tendency to approach playmates through a common interest in toys and other objects
- the pleasure derived through the symmetrical rhythm of turn-taking with toys and other objects
- the insistence of peers and parents that objects be divided and shared when possible
- the child's natural empathetic response to another child who may desire a turn or share, bolstered by the adult's reasoned message that the other child will be unhappy in the absence of sharing
- the child's pragmatic desires to stay in the good graces of a playmate out of an expectation that the playmate [or sibling] will reciprocate

Eventually the child will come to understand concepts like fairness and distributive justice resulting in a greater consistency and generosity in sharing.

Often if you put your kids in charge of sharing, they will come up with novel ways that you'd never think of. "I'll sit in the front seat with Mom on odd-numbered days and you can have it on even-numbered days."

## Strategy #22: Stay out of their fights.

Fighting between siblings is a perennial problem. Kids fight for lots of different reasons—over property, over territory, because they're frustrated with themselves or a friend and need a punching bag, or even because they're bored and have nothing better to do. And sometimes they're even enjoying it. Whatever the reason, you can either become skilled at handling the situation when your children are fighting or you can make it worse. There are a number of knee-jerk statements that almost all of us have made at one time or another, and they're totally useless in solving the problems. They include:

- Stop it!
- Shame on you two!
- Who started this?
- I don't care how this started. I want it stopped right now.
- You two are driving me crazy (giving me gray hair, giving me an ulcer).
- You're too old for this kind of behavior.
- You should know better.

These comments, rather than solving a problem, usually reinforce your impotence in the whole situation.

Sometimes, if the fighting is the kind of harmless bickering that is meant to irritate and upset you, the best response is no response. Ignore the behavior and tell yourself that your children are having an important experience in conflict resolution.

If the situation escalates, however, and adult intervention is necessary, begin by acknowledging your children's anger. Be sure that you accurately reflect each child's point of view and describe the problem with respect. Now, here's the tough part that will take practice: Express confidence in your children's ability to find their own solution and leave the room. If your children are in danger of seriously hurting each other or the environment, remain calm. Describe what you see. "I see a situation where two people are very angry with each other and could injure each other. I'm going to separate you for a few minutes while you cool down. Then we can talk."

When your kids are fighting out of sheer boredom and meanness, try just leaving the scene. I used to go into the bathroom with a book, shut the door and lock it, and refuse to come out until all was quiet on the western front. This same technique works very well in the car. Simply pull over to the side of the road and get out. Tell them you'll be back when they stop fighting. This is an especially effective technique if you're taking them someplace they really want to go like a birthday party or vacation. I've even heard of some bus drivers using this technique, although I'm not sure what I would have done if one of my school bus drivers had deserted a sinking ship (or an out-of-control school bus).

## Strategy #23: Model how to apologize.

Children need models for how to handle conflict. Integrate these statements in your family relationships, and help your children to use them when appropriate.

- I never knew you felt that way.
- I didn't realize you would take it the way you did.
- I would have acted differently had I known.
- I wish you had said something.
- I had no idea you were sensitive about the subject.
- I admit I was wrong. Can you forgive me?

## Strategy #24: Play it again, Sam.

Set up a tape recorder at the scene of the battle (e.g., the kitchen, the family room, a child's bedroom) and then push play. Although I haven't tried this method with my own children, I have used it in the classroom and know parents who have used it successfully. Playing back a tape of sibling battles for the participants to hear may give them a new perspective and provide an opportunity for discussion and problem solving.

## Strategy #25: Tell a story.

I'm a big believer in the power of stories to move and change children. Find books that feature the virtues of family loyalty, friendship, and positive relationships between siblings to read aloud to your children. Or make up your own stories.

## Strategy #26: Act it out.

In role playing, two or more individuals act out a brief scene from a hypothetical situation. Role playing can create a family atmosphere of experimentation and creativity and will often help the entire communication process. Role playing can help children learn to disagree without being disagreeable.

## Strategy #27: Talk it out.

Small-group discussion is an age-old methodology. It has been defined as face-to-face mutual interchange of ideas and opinions between members of a relatively small group. Your family is the original small group. This process is best used when the group has an idea, concern, or issue that is worthy of discussion. If you're not ready to try a regular family council, then everyone should at least "talk about it" once in a while. Make sure to have big sheets of paper for recording the "group memory." We used to have our group discussions in a restaurant that used white butcher paper for tablecloths. They furnished jars of crayons with which diners could write. We took notes on the "tablecloth," and that helped us keep track of our discussion.

The leader of the group must model behaviors that are critical to the success of small-group discussion:

- Encourage the expression of ideas by all members of the group.
- Establish and maintain an informal, cooperative, and permissive group climate.
- Make suggestions instead of giving directions.
- When necessary, use humor to enliven the atmosphere.

At the end of the meeting, summarize the results. If there are tasks or assignments to be completed, make sure they are written down and everyone agrees.

## Strategy #28: Work on temper control.

If your children have a difficult time controlling violent outbursts of anger and temper, teach and model temper control strategies for them:

- Immediately focus on something else or someone else in the house. Try to divert attention elsewhere for a few minutes to give yourself a break.
- Count to ten slowly before making any move. Take deep relaxing breaths, and try to regain control of your emotions.
- Ask yourself if it is worth getting hurt or hurting your sibling over this matter.

## Strategy #29: Use reverse psychology.

I've tried this technique with students in my elementary school, but it must be used wisely. Here's how it works. Johnny has decorated the bathroom walls with grafitti. The consequences are simple. He stays after school and decorates the bathroom walls with more grafitti. Then he washes it all off. Sometimes a little "gross exaggeration" and humor can help children see just how ridiculous their behavior has become. Use your best judgment.

## Strategy #30: Try mind mapping.

"Mind mapping" is a process that can tap the creativity and problem-solving abilities of those individuals who think visually rather than verbally. Write an issue, problem, or situation in a circle in the center of a large piece of paper (butcher paper or chart paper works best), and then draw branches out from the center and label them with major headings. As ideas related to each category occur, smaller circles are drawn and the ideas written there. Hang your mind map on the refrigerator or a bulletin board so family members can add ideas to it. Here's an example of a mind map that one family generated to help them solve the problem of "borrowing without asking."

## Strategy #31: Employ cooperative groups.

Cooperative groups help children learn that together we are smarter, stronger, and faster than we are alone. I like to use a game like Boggle to demonstrate the power of a cooperative group. In this game, individuals compete against each other to find words on a grid of letters. I am always amazed at the number of different words each person can find. When all of the words are considered collectively, they always exceed the number that any one individual was able to discover on his/her own. Cooperative groups are good for doing jobs like cleaning the garage, making dinner, getting the yard cleaned up for spring, or organizing the family photo albums.

## Strategy #32: Have a group conversation.

Group conversation is a process that has been used in community groups to bring people together who traditionally have encountered barriers and roadblocks because of their differing ages, races, social status, ethnic backgrounds, religious backgrounds, economic levels, and educational levels. This same process can be used in your family if you are experiencing conflicts and rivalries. Conversations should focus on topics that will develop interpersonal connections rather than solving specific problems. Here are some ideas for topics:

- The Best Vacation You've Ever Had
- My Favorite Foods
- The Best Present I've Ever Gotten
- If I Were an Animal, I'd Like to Be . . .

## Strategy #33: Identify "air time."

Air time is a process that makes sure everyone has an equal amount of time to share concerns or give an opinion. If you have family members who monopolize discussions or take too much of the available "air time," structure your family meetings or problem-solving sessions using a timer to make sure that everyone gets equal time.

## Strategy #34: Seek outside help.

Family therapy or parenting classes are two options to consider when nothing else is working. An objective outsider can usually see our life situation more clearly than we can, and from their background and experience offer advice to help us cope with sibling rivalry. There may be deeper family issues, of which we are unaware, that will emerge in counseling or therapy, particularly if the situation is complicated by stepsiblings, a sibling with disabilities, or marital conflict.

## Strategy #35: Pop "The Question."

The chairperson asks each family member "The Question" (this assignment can rotate from meal to meal). The question can vary, but here are some examples:

- What do you like about yourself?
- What do you feel good about today?
- What are you happy about?
- What are you improving at?

## Strategy #36: Sit on the bench.

Sometimes when two siblings are in the thick of battle, you can help them solve their differences by placing them side by side on a picnic or piano bench. Tell them they cannot leave the bench until each confesses to the other person (and their parents) what they did wrong, and vice versa.

## Strategy #37: Think chairs.

If siblings are too emotionally involved in an argument or battle to solve their differences immediately (see Strategy #49), put them each in a separate chair at some distance from one another and give them time to cool down and think through how they will solve their problem. After the cool-off period, place them on a bench to find a compromise or solution.

### Endnotes

1. Stephen and Marianne Garber, *Good Behavior: Over 1200 Solutions to Your Child's Problems from Birth to Age 12* (New York: Villard Books, 1987).

2. Thomas Gordon, *Discipline that Works* (New York: Plume, 1991).

3. William Damon, *The Moral Child: Nurturing Children's Natural Moral Growth* (New York: Free Press, 1988), p. 49.

# 5

# Activities to Nurture Supportive Siblings

**E**ven though I'd endured my own share of sibling battles with my younger brother and sister, I just knew that when I had my own children, everything would be different. *I'd* be able to raise perfect children who loved each other, seldom said unkind things, and almost never fought. Of course, this was not the case. But I did find throughout my years of parenting that whenever I took a proactive stance, my days were happier. When I planned ahead and worked with my children to encourage them and facilitate their differences, we came much closer to our vision of a "happy family." The suggestions for nurturing supportive siblings that follow are a compilation of things that have worked for me and other families. Choose the ones that fit the needs of your family.

## Strategy #1: [Not] Too Many Cooks

There is an old saying that "too many cooks spoil the broth," but I haven't found that to be true in my kitchen. According to Christopher Kimball, the editor of *Cook's Illustrated,* cooking is perhaps our last opportunity to work together as a family. Preparing a meal together or making a special dessert for someone's birthday can illustrate for kids the adage that many hands make light work. When siblings work side by side in the kitchen (in the garden, on the workbench) they will learn to depend on each other and work together. Of course you will need to be prepared for a somewhat messier kitchen than if you were working alone. Give each person a job that matches his maturity and abilities.

## Strategy #2: Invite a Friend to Dinner

When each family member takes turns inviting a friend over for the evening meal, all kinds of wonderful things can happen. This special dinner, held once every two weeks, will foster good communication and relationships for everyone. More importantly, however, each child will have an opportunity to "shine" in his or her own family setting. Make sure that parents invite their friends also.

## Strategy #3: The Family Journal

You can compile your family journal in many places— a three-ring binder, a spiral notebook, or a special hardback book with blank pages. The important thing is that every member of the family contribute to it regularly. Preschoolers will need to draw or dictate their journal entries. Journal entries consist of one or two sentences. They can be observations about the world, things that happened to you during the day, or special messages to other family members. Keep the journal in a handy place. Take time once or twice a week to read aloud all of the entries.

## Strategy #4: The Family Bulletin Board

Our refrigerator functioned as the bulletin board when my children were growing up. It contained art work, certificates, messages, special photos, and a calendar of upcoming events. Although we sometimes had to fight our way through the clutter to get a glass of milk, it was worth it. Everyone got equal billing on the refrigerator and we periodically changed the display to keep it fresh. Other families use a cork bulletin board to display their special family memorabilia.

## Strategy #5: And the Winner Is . . .

I once heard about an organization where a rubber chicken was rotated from branch office to branch office, the "winner" being the office with the lowest sales quota for the month. Nobody needs that kind of reinforcement, but the idea of a rotating trophy or sign that commends a specific child for his/her kindness, empathy, and understanding during a given period of time might just encourage your children to be on their best behavior. You'll need to hold a family meeting to talk about the ground rules and how the winner will be chosen (e.g., Mom or Dad will nominate or all family members vote). Just make sure the same child doesn't always win the prize!

## Strategy #6: Team Spirit

You can build team spirit in your family in many ways. Make it a daily part of your family life. Write a family chant or cheer; develop a family motto; take "team pictures"; publish a family newspaper at Christmas to send out to family and friends; or adopt a child or family with whom to share your family's blessings.

## Strategy #7: Open for Business

Sibling relationships were always at their best at our house when Emily and Patrick were collaborating on a joint business venture. Once or twice a year they put together the proverbial lemonade stand. Once they collected their old toys and had their own garage sale. Other families work together on a "real" money-making venture. One large family we knew teamed up to do newspaper delivery. Different family members delivered on different mornings. That way everyone got to sleep in once in a while. Other possibilities for a family business: lawn mowing and yard care, pet-sitting, or house cleaning.

## Strategy #8: Being a Good Sport

We enjoy taking our grandchildren bowling and encourage them to support and cheer each other on. With the help of bumpers on either side of the alley, even the youngest is able to get an occasional strike or spare. The goal is not to get the highest score, but to improve your own score from game to game. Your children will only care about sportsmanship if you teach them. The real goal is self-improvement, and cheating, tantrums, fighting, and a "sour-grapes" attitude just aren't acceptable. Always talk about good sportsmanship before heading out to play.

## Strategy #9: Family "Time Capsule"

Put together a time capsule that includes a representative sampling of things from every family member. Store the items in a sturdy cardboard box or container and put it away in the attic or a high closet shelf for the year. Possible items to include in the capsule are: snapshots, handwriting samples, favorite candy wrapper, a short letter from Mom or Dad describing the child, a short essay on what I want to be when I grow up, or a list of current favorite activities and friends. This is a good activity to do at the end of summer vacation, before school starts, or on New Year's Day. Younger children may have a difficult time with the time capsule concept and want to open up the box much sooner. Use your own judgment!

## Strategy #10: Family Shield

Bob Keeshan, a.k.a. Captain Kangaroo, gives a wonderful suggestion in his *Family Fun Book*[1]—making a special Family Shield, decorated with a picture that represents your family. He suggests using poster board and tracing a large circle with a dinner plate. If you want your shield to be larger, use a small round tray or a pizza pan. Use markers, crayons, or any other materials you have around the home to construct your shield. Draw pictures of your house and family pets. Write your family name on the shield, and when you're finished, hang it in a prominent place in your home.

## Strategy #11: Family Photo Display

When my first husband died, someone suggested that we put together a display of pictures and memorabilia to display at the wake. We mounted them on a piece of masonite board covered with cloth. I was unprepared for how enthusiastic the children would be at the prospect of such a task. They worked together sorting through the pictures and remembering happy times. At the time, I wished we'd done a family photo display much sooner. Going through old photographs is a wonderful way to talk about collective memories and bond as a family. Ask your child about memories he/she has about earlier times.

## Strategy #12: The Family Tree

Rabbi Neil Kurshan, in his delightful little book *Raising Your Child to Be a Mensch*,[2] tells the story of a family that keeps a large picture of a tree in their living room. (You could put yours on the refrigerator or a bulletin board as well.) Whenever a family member demonstrates kindness, responsibility, or another admirable character trait, a leaf noting the event is placed on the tree.

## Strategy #13: The Unhurried Child

David Elkind, in his book *The Hurried Child*,[3] bemoans the pace at which we expect children to move through life. We want them to be all grown-up before they're ready for junior high. Hurry and hubbub also exacerbate sibling rivalry. Here are some ways to eliminate hurry in your house, suggested by Richard Carlson in *Celebrate Your Child: The Art of Happy Parenting*[4]:

- Be patient. Think about how often you hurry your children . . . to get ready . . . to eat breakfast . . . to answer your questions.
- Schedule nonstructured time. Kids need time to just "be."
- Encourage alone time. Having time and space to "do your own thing" will help your child get to know himself or herself.
- Celebrate silence. Turn off the radio, the TV, and the CD player, and just enjoy the beauty of silence.

## Strategy #14: Room Redecorations

When siblings share a bedroom, rivalry can become especially intense. One way to alleviate some of the tenseness is to permit the children to rearrange and redecorate the room. Of course, you can't just turn them loose. Before you begin, develop some ground rules and help them negotiate the sticky points of the decorating project.

## Strategy #15: Smiley Faces for Good Behavior

Many schools use this behavior model, and it works well on the home front as well. Make a batch of smiling and frowning faces on a sheet of 8½-x-11" paper. Photocopy the sheet and cut out the smiley faces. Whenever you "catch" your children being cooperative and good with one another, toss a smiley face into a basket or box. Whenever your children are fighting or arguing, put in a frowning face. At the end of a specified period of time, if there are more smiles than frowns, the family will do something special together like go out for pizza or go bowling. Take time before you begin this activity to make a list of all the positive things that deserve smiley faces and all the negative things that deserve frowning faces.

## Strategy #16: Family Message Center

Imagine my surprise when I recently called the branch of our family in Minnesota. The message on the answering machine instructed me to choose one of several different numbers for each family member. After pushing the number that I wanted I heard a message from that individual and was instructed to leave my message. There was even a number for Baby Elizabeth (just five weeks old). Her message consisted of some hearty background crying, but there was an opportunity to leave a message of love for the baby. If you're not as high-tech as our family in Minnesota, put a message together that gives every family member a chance to participate.

## Strategy #17: The Hall of Fame

Even if you don't have a spare hallway in your home in which to hang family pictures, set aside a spot on a piano or table to place small framed pictures. Display pictures of grandparents or even great-grandparents and talk about their unique attributes and accomplishments in the family. My children always enjoyed hearing about my "Uncle Babe." The baby of his family, he spent his spare time as a clown, appearing in parades and visiting nursing homes and hospitals. My favorite photo shows him charming my younger cousins.

## Strategy #18: More Blessed to Give

Designate one or two weeks (or more if you like) out of every month as Sharing and Caring Week. During this week each family member will choose a special project to do for someone else. Shovel the walk or mow the lawn for a disabled neighbor, call a friend who is shut in, help a younger sibling with a difficult school project.

## Strategy #19: Monthly Family Calendar

I'm already collecting the pictures to use on the family calendar for next year. We'll be giving it as a gift to our children and grandchildren. January will show Grandma and Grandpa at Baby Elizabeth's baptism. February will show us standing beside our backyard fountain enjoying the desert plantings while everyone else in the family is cold and frozen. In March we'll be at a retreat in the Allegheny Mountains of Pennsylvania. And so the year goes. Buy some film and start to plan your family calendar now. Your children can even develop a kids' calendar to send to their grandparents, aunts, and uncles. Printing shops with color copy capabilities offer the calendar option at a reasonable price.

## Strategy #20: Tell Me a Story

Look in the library's card catalog under the subject heading "sibling rivalry," and read about how some fictional characters cope with the ups and downs of brothers and sisters getting along. There are dozens of good titles. Your library will have its own collection.

## Strategy #21: Family Stationery

Use a computer program like Print Shop Deluxe to design your own family greeting cards. Encourage your children to send birthday cards to siblings and other relatives. Suggest they send thank-you notes to everyone who gives them a gift.

## Strategy #22: Giving Gifts

Help even the youngest members of your family to shop for birthday and Christmas gifts for one another.

As your children mature and begin to earn money of their own, they will be skilled at picking out and giving gifts to one another. Don't expect gift giving to come naturally. You will need to nurture and encourage the giving spirit.

## Strategy #23: Publishing a Family Newspaper

If you're computer literate at your house, use one of the wonderful desktop publishing programs to publish your own family newspaper. Appoint an editor (parent or older sibling) and then begin taking submissions to the newspaper. Even the youngest can make a contribution. Make copies of the paper and send them to relatives and friends.

## Strategy #24: Sibling Secrets

Whether it's planning breakfast in bed for Mom on her birthday or decorating Dad's bathroom for Father's Day, kids love to surprise their parents. Stimulate teamwork and cooperation. Send them out shopping together for a single gift.

## Strategy #25: Growing Closer

Working together to plant, cultivate, harvest, and preserve is a family project that can instill perseverance and togetherness. From choosing the seeds to harvesting the fruits, gardening is real work that will bring children closer to each other. Sometimes several families in a neighborhood can work together on one plot.

# Strategy #26: Neighborhood Fun

Help your children to plan and play together. Consider outdoor activities that encourage cooperation and family fun, such as a backyard carnival to raise money for a charity, or building a treehouse or play-house.

# Strategy #27: Make a Video

Have your kids put their heads together to write and make a video on sibling rivalry. They could include the worst things brothers and sisters do to bug each other and suggestions for parents on how to get their kids to get along better.

# Strategy #28: Do Not Disturb

All kids need a little privacy. Help your children to understand the concept of boundaries, and teach them to respect the privacy of their siblings. My son had a sign like the ones in hotels that announced when he didn't want to be disturbed. The rest of the family respected his wishes, and he was a lot more pleasant when he'd had a little solitude in his room. If your children share bedrooms, develop a privacy plan that gives each child some time alone.

# Strategy #29: You're Bugging Me

Denise Champman Weston and Mark S. Weston, in their book *Playful Parenting,* suggest making fuzzy bugs out of yarn and putting a bunch of them in a bowl in the kitchen.[5] Anytime someone in the family does something irritating to another person, the one who does the irritating is given a bug and told "you're bugging me." This method can reduce aggressiveness, hostility, name-calling, and fighting.

## Strategy #30: The Team Chore Chart

The Westons also suggest a new twist to the time-honored American tradition, the chore chart.[6] This one contains a new wrinkle—a rotation of chores each day so that all chores are done by almost every person during the week. The team (family) will win an award at the end of the week if everyone does his or her part on every day.

## Strategy #31: Doesn't Belong Box and Auction

Another wonderful idea suggested by the Westons will help your children be more reponsible for their own and other's belongings.[7] Any time a family member uses or plays with something that needs to be put away, he/she can put it in its proper place or put it in the Doesn't Belong Box.

Similarly, if another family member sees an object that has not been put away, he or she can put it in the box. At the end of the day, everyone looks inside the box, sees if anything there belongs to them, removes the object, and puts it where it belongs. The logical consequence of not putting away your things at the end of the day is that they will be put aside for an auction two or three days later. At the auction, the owner of the item needs to buy back his possessions by offering services such as doing extra chores or a good deed for a sibling or parent. You may need to make an exception for schoolbooks and essential objects.

## Strategy #32: It's My Right

One can scarcely read the newspaper or watch television without hearing a group loudly proclaiming that their rights have been violated. Our children often falsely believe that they should get whatever they want regardless of the consequences to the rest of the family. Begin early to teach your children the following important lessons about rights:

- Everyone has a right to his or her own opinion.
- Just because something is important to you doesn't automatically mean that others must sacrifice what is important to them.
- People have a right to be who they are, even if it's not who we want them to be.
- People have the right to make mistakes.

## Strategy #33: Rights of Ownership

Schulman and Mekler set forth the following rights of ownership in their book *Bringing Up a Moral Child*.[8] Explaining these rights and constantly teaching them to your children will help avoid fights and arguments over "things."

- The person who owns an object has the right to determine who will use it and for how long.

- When you agree to let someone use something of yours, keep your word.
- When an object is public property, such as a playground swing or a school ball, who uses it is usually determined on a first-come, first-served basis.
- Sometimes, if a lot of children want to use the same thing at the same time, time limits are placed on use so that everyone takes a turn and gets a chance to enjoy it.
- Sometimes some special skill or personal characteristic earns one special privileges. For instance, in a game, the previous high scorer (or low scorer) might have the right to go first the second time around.

## Strategy #34: Owning Your Own Feelings

How often have you refused to let your children own their own feelings? I'm still tempted to do so when my twenty-somethings call to tell me they're discouraged, depressed, or lonely. I immediately want to disagree with them and try to talk them out of how they're feeling. That's not what they need. They may need help in working through their feelings, but the last thing they need is someone telling them to pretend or repress how they're really feeling.

When a child says he's mad at a brother or sister, don't tell him he isn't really angry. Now, letting a child own his feelings doesn't mean you'll let him do anything he wants. It simply means you're giving him permission to be who he is in psychological safety.

## Strategy #35: The Kid Book

Many children begin life with a baby book. If that child is a first-born, the entries are copious and detailed, including locks of hair, hand and footprints and the names and addresses of everyone who sent baby gifts. As the family circle grows, there is less time to fill in the first word and paste in the first tooth. Once you've reached the mark where the baby book no longer will hold any more (usually around the age of seven), start another book for your child. A blank scrapbook will do very nicely. Save special things for this "kid book," like letters from Grandma, stories and artwork, programs and ticket stubs, invitations and newspaper clippings. We put our memories in a large box that was covered with attractive contact paper. While it wasn't as well organized as a scrapbook, it served the same purpose. Our children knew that their life was being chronicled and collected. They counted! One of my good friends, a professional photographer by trade, gave each of her children a wonderful gift when they turned thirteen. She had choice photographs enlarged and mounted on heavy board and then had them bound into a book with the child's name embossed on the front cover. It's a marvelous treasure.

## Strategy #36: The Family Book

Do the same thing for your family as you do for each child. Collect photographs, memorabilia, letters and notes, and all of those other special things that make your family unique.

# Strategy #37: My Favorite Meal

Once a week, let one family member choose his or her favorite meal. My grandson Brian has a limited repertoire of favorite foods (crab legs and macaroni and cheese), but when one or the other is served, he feels very special.

# Strategy #38: Morning Announcements

To keep the lines of communication open in your family, institute morning announcements. These are a little like the morning announcements often found in schools, where someone reads off a list of activities and special events for the day. For your "home-grown" version, make sure each family member tells the rest of the family what is going on in his or her day. Dad may have an important meeting. Mom may have a deadline for a critical project. Sister Sue may have a field trip to the science museum during the day and a birthday party after school, and Brother Brian may be worried about the big basketball game. If members of your family are like ships passing in the night with little or no awareness of what is going on in each other's lives, then start making morning announcements.

# Strategy #39: Small Talk

Small talk is an important social convention—the ability to chat about inconsequential and relatively unimportant topics as conversational transitions. The weather, sports, travel, family happenings, and the like are subjects for small talk. Small talk bridges the gap between awkward silence and moving on to more meaningful conversation. Small talk takes place when you encounter people in shopping malls, run into them after church, or see them at the health club. Modeling and practicing small talk at the dinner table will help reduce those sibling arguments.

## Endnotes

1. Bob Keeshan, *Family Fun Activity Book* (Minneapolis: Deaconess Press, 1994).

2. Neil Kurshan, *Raising Your Child to Be a Mensch* (New York: Atheneum, 1987).

3. David Elkind, *The Hurried Child* (Reading, Mass.: Addison Wesley, 1988).

4. Richard Carlson, *Celebrate Your Child: The Art of Happy Parenting* (San Rafael, Calif.: New World Library, 1992).

5. Denise Champman Weston and Mark S. Weston, *Playful Parenting: Turning the Dilemma of Discipline into Fun and Games* (New York: G.P. Putnam's Sons, 1993), p. 80.

6. Ibid., p. 102.

7. Ibid., p. 106.

8. Michael Schulman and Evan Mekler, *Bringing Up a Moral Child* (New York: Doubleday, 1994), pp. 213-214.

# 6

# What to Do about Special Situations

**F**acilitating and managing sibling rivalry in the "average" family (if those really do exist anymore) is often a challenge. But stir in some stepsiblings or a brother or sister with a disability (e.g., learning, physical, ADHD) and parents will likely need extra measures of wisdom, patience, and problem-solving abilities.

## Stepsiblings

Our Minnesota grandchildren, Julie (15), Steve (14), and Brian (12), are outstanding examples of how young people can handle the blending of a family. In just two years, they've acquired a new stepmother and a half sister (newborn). Those of us who grew up negotiating our way through relationships with one set of siblings might well step back in awe as we watch the adaptability, flexibility, and enthusiasm with which these three have adjusted to a new family constellation in a relatively short period of time. They didn't ask for these changes and had no choice in the matter, but they're amazingly resilient.

But there's no doubt that multiple questions and concerns have occupied their young minds as they've attempted to make sense out of all that has happened to them. Questions and thoughts like the following are only natural.

- Is she being nice to me because she married my dad and wants to show him that she is a good mother, or does she really like me for myself?
- Did Dad marry her because he loves her or because he feels we need a mother to raise us?
- Will my dad and stepmom love the new baby more than they love me?

There are some important qualities present in their home, however, that have helped this transition to be a smooth one. They include open communication, participation and democracy, and a sense of security and being loved.

Those children are going to need all of the above and more. Even though the Brady Bunch did it, it's hard for some parents to love their stepchildren as if they were their own and even harder for stepchildren to return that love. Even when natural parents have been abusive, neglectful, and inadequate, they are the "real thing." All children secretly believe, or at least hope, that their estranged parents will someday reunite. Remarriage removes that hope, and in too many cases the feelings of regret, anger, and hostility kick in.

Author Kevin Leman suggests another possible source of sibling problems when families are blended: birth order. Former perfectionistic, organized, and top-of-the-heap firstborns may suddenly find themselves displaced by an older firstborn. Babies of the family (like my grandson, Brian) may suddenly find a new "baby" on the scene. Reading Leman's book if you're blending your family will provide some useful and amusing insights.

Here are some recommended readings for helping your blended family get off to a good start.

- Barnes, Robert. *You're Not My Daddy*. Dallas: Word Publishing, 1992.
- Berman, Claire. *Making It As a Stepparent*. New York: Harper and Row, 1986.
- Bloomfield, Harold. *Making Peace in Your Stepfamily*. New York: Hyperion, 1993.
- Brown, Beth. *When You're Mom No. 2*. Ann Arbor, Mich.: Servant Publications, 1991.
- Leman, Kevin. *Living in a Step-Family without Getting Stepped On*. Nashville: Thomas Nelson, 1994.

## Siblings with Attention Deficit Disorder

Jason is a seven-year-old first grader. Recently diagnosed with ADHD (Attention Deficit Hyperactivity Disorder), he has never enjoyed particularly good relations with his two older siblings, a sister who is twelve and a nine-year-old brother. His hyperactivity and impulsivity seemed to monopolize their parents' attention. He wouldn't stay out of his siblings' rooms, broke their belongings with regularity, and continually pestered them when they were watching TV. They called him a "brat," and frequently conspired to get him into trouble.

Now on medication, Jason's out-of-control behavior is beginning to moderate. His parents have become more sensitive to the dynamics of parenting a child with ADHD and are working with Jason's siblings to educate them about how best to handle their brother's behavior. Telling siblings to ignore the child with ADHD isn't good advice. Sometimes the best way to handle the situation is for the bothered sibling to stop what he/she is doing for a minute or two to give the child with ADHD some attention and then to let him or her know, "Now I need to get back to my homework . . . or model building . . . or computer game."

Jason's parents have taught the older siblings a simple four-step process for children (or adults) to use if Jason becomes intrusive or interruptive:

- Stop whatever you are doing and look directly into the child's eyes.
- Ask him/her what he/she wants.
- If possible, make a deal in which you let him/her have his/her way, to some extent, in exchange for no longer interrupting you.
- End the conversation with a firm statement of exactly what you want; for example, that he not pester you.

Siblings of children with ADHD may consider their parents too supportive of the ADHD child and may become angry at their total absorption and commitment. The child with ADHD will frequently violate restrictions, limits, and guidelines and appear to get away with a lot. Siblings of children with ADHD will need special coping skills to handle the frustration that can often build up over perceived inequities and feelings of guilt. Parents should try to help siblings understand the plight of the ADHD child by providing explanations or reading material. Sometimes an older sibling can benefit from doing a school research project on topics concerning ADHD.

Maintaining consistency in the treatment and discipline of all children in the family when one or more of the children has ADHD is difficult. Some parents, in their attempts to avoid favoritism, fall into arbitrary traps of consistency, which in reality cause more stress and disharmony than an honest appraisal of the situation and a little truth. You can't possibly treat your child with ADHD and your non-ADHD children the same. They handle responsibilities differently; they are different ages; they are developmentally different. And you will be different in your approach to parenting at different points in your life. More important than artificial consistency are *congruence* and *contemporaneous treatment*.

*Congruence* means matching your feelings and your actions—giving your children honest appraisals of how their behavior has made you feel and what the impact will be. We are human beings and our sleep, nutrition, stress levels, and work demands vary greatly. It's OK to "lose it" once in a while if you respond with honesty and clarity to your child. "I'm sorry I was cross with you. We're not going out for ice cream right now. I feel the way I do because you said some nasty things to me. I'm going to sit in my time-out chair for a while and catch my breath. Maybe we'll go for ice cream in a little while."

*Contemporaneous treatment* is treatment according to the readiness and developmental level of your child. Treat your child according to his/her readiness to engage in an activity or handle a responsibility, regardless of what you would do with another child. It's OK to tell a second child, "When you're ready to handle this kind of responsibility, I'll let you do the same thing." Penalizing one child for the inability of another child to handle something is not fair.

Make sure that you give your non-ADHD children time to have their friends over without the ADHD child around and that you provide a safe place for your non-ADHD children to store their belongings.

Families that are able to use the problem-solving processes mentioned in earlier chapters and talk out conflicts in family meetings will handle sibling rivalry with far less difficulty. If your children can learn to express their feelings in calm, but assertive ways rather than screaming, whining, hitting, grabbing, and teasing, your family climate will be much less stressful. Ignoring the problem, however, will not make it go away!

Consult these resources for further information:

Kenney, Patricia; Terdal, Leif; and Fusetti, Lydia. *The Hyperactive Child Book.* New York: St. Martin's Press, 1993.

McEwan, Elaine K. *Attention Deficit Disorder.* Wheaton, Ill.: Harold Shaw Publishers, 1995.

# Siblings with Mental or Physical Disabilities

The anticipation of the birth of a new brother or sister is an exciting time. But when that child is born with a physical or mental handicap, time stands still for everyone. The siblings are usually ignored as Mom, Dad, and the extended family spend days and nights at the hospital trying to find out what's wrong. Feelings of guilt, pain, isolation, and sometimes anger swirl around the siblings. Siblings can take one of two approaches to this traumatic situation: either choose to be "very, very good," or begin acting out in an immediate demand for attention. Although the "very, very good approach" is certainly easier for parents to handle in the short run, these well-behaved siblings often harbor anger and resentment at the neglect they suffered in the early years of a sibling's birth.

A child with mental retardation is very different from the other children in your family. He learns more slowly and with greater difficulty, and there may even come a time when a younger sibling will outpace the retarded sibling's accomplishments. But your mentally disabled child's differences will not keep him/her from being a loved and important part of the family. And the same is true of children with physical handicaps. Although they will often require special equipment, automobiles, and even modified houses, they will bring your children the opportunity to develop empathy, caring, and love.

Studies show that having a brother or sister with mental disabilities often has a positive effect on other children over both the long and short term. For one thing, siblings of children with handicaps tend to have a wider variety of friends than other children. Children who are close to a brother or sister with mental retardation are also more likely to embrace humanitarian life goals—to be concerned with issues like justice, equality, and compassion. However, many questions and concerns will also arise. Here are some typical reactions from siblings of different ages.

**Preschoolers** may resent the extra time you spend with a disabled sibling, and they may suddenly regress to an earlier developmental stage in an attempt to get your attetion. Capitalize on their desires to be helpful and work on building relationships.

**School-age children** may worry about "catching" mental retardation. They may be embarasssed at being seen in public with a sibling who is physically disabled, or they may overcompensate with achievement to help you make up for what they see as your "loss."

**Adolescents** may be angry, embarassed, or have a real fear of being responsible for the child.

At any age, siblings of handicapped children can demonstrate any or all of a variety of emotional responses:

- a strong sense of responsibility for the handicapped sibling
- a misunderstanding of the actual severity of the handicap
- anger at parents for giving all of their love and attention to the disabed sibling
- resentment at the time and money allocated to the handicapped sibling

Here are some suggestions from parents of disabled children who have successfully handled the stresses of managing sibling rivalry in this setting:

**Try to schedule one-on-one time** with your non-handicapped child every day. Even if this time period is no more than ten or fifteen minutes, give your child this much-needed extra love and attention.

**Don't hesitate to talk about** the handicapped child and answer any questions your other children may have. Encourage your children to put their thoughts and questions into words. Discussion will help to ease their anxieties. Try talking to the children at bedtime, as that is sometimes a quiet, nonthreatening opportunity for serious conversations. Supply your children with accurate information that is appropriate to their age level. If you don't know the answers, find them. Willingly volunteer information so that your children will be less likely to see their sibling's disability as a "family secret."

**Help your child empathize** with the disabled child and learn how to express those feelings in a direct way. Model statements like the following for your nonhandicapped child:

- I feel your fear in doing this.
- I can understand your frustration in getting this done.
- I can imagine the pain you are feeling.
- I realize your anxiety.

Conversely, help your child learn to share the moments of extraordinary happiness that everyone feels when a milestone is reached or a goal is accomplished. Model statements like these:

- I share your joy.
- I feel your excitement.
- I understand your happiness.

**Involve your nondisabled children** with your disabled child. They can teach a mentally disabled child or help a physically challenged child get around. Make sure, however, that siblings understand that it is not their job to teach or supervise their disabled sibling. Encourage participation through love and care.

**Affirm your nondisabled children** for the love and care they give to a sibling. Empathize with a difficulty they might have had in getting a sibling home from school or off the special bus.

**Don't expect your nondisabled child to be the "wonderful one."** Kids deserve the right to be ordinary and have their ordinary needs be just as important as the child with the problem. Beware of the vicious cycle that can be created when you begin to make more demands on the other children in your family to compensate for the child who is disabled. The needs of the nondisabled sibling are brushed aside, and then he/she begins to resent the disabled child.

Here are three excellent books to give you additional help:

Dickman, Irving, with Dr. Sol Gordon. *One Miracle at a Time: Getting Help for a Child with a Disability.* New York: Simon and Schuster, 1993.

Smith, Romayne. *Children with Mental Retardation: A Parents' Guide*. Rockville, Md.: Woodbine House, 1993.

Thompson, Charlotte. *Raising a Handicapped Child*. New York: William Morrow, 1986.

## Siblings with Learning Disabilities

Explaining what a learning disability is to the siblings of a child who has one may be more challenging than explaining mental and physical disabilities or Attention Deficit Disorder. The symptoms are more subtle and often show up only in the school setting. Siblings may not "see" anything wrong with a brother and sister and fail to understand how somebody who seems "pretty smart" has such a hard time learning his spelling words or writing a report. Siblings may grow resentful of the extra time that is given to help with school work. The learning-disabled child will often work very hard for less than perfect grades while a brother or sister will sail through the curriculum with little or no effort. Parents must work very hard at making each child feel unique and appreciated for his/her special talents and gifts (see chapter 3).

Consult these resources for additional help:

Tuttle, Cheryl Gerson, and Paquette, Penny. *Parenting a Child with a Learning Disability*. Chicago: Contemporary Books, 1993.

Weiss, Elizabeth. *Mothers Talk about Learning Disabilities*. Englewood Cliffs, N.J.: Prentice-Hall, 1989.

Whatever the makeup of your family, you have what it takes to make it run smoothly. Just remember these steps to successful sibling relationships:

1. Encourage shared decision making and cooperative family activities.
2. Make everyone accountable for their actions.
3. Keep those lines of communication open.
4. Make each of your children feels unique and valued, no matter what his or her abilities or disabilities.
5. If you want to change your kids' behavior, just remember to check out your own. Before pointing the finger at anyone, take a personal inventory.

Siblings of children with special needs have an extra challenge and also an extra opportunity. Many of them grow up to be understanding, mature people who have a unique ability to accept people who are different from themselves. All our children would benefit from that gift!